Mediterranean Diet Cookbook

Delicious and Nutritious Recipes for Optimal Health

Thanos Georgiou

Copyright © 2023 - All rights reserved.

The content contained within this book may not be reproduced, duplicated, or transmitted without direct written permission from the author or the publisher.

Under no circumstances will any blame or legal responsibility be held against the publisher, or author, for any damages, reparation, or monetary loss due to the information contained within this book. Either directly or indirectly.

Legal Notice:

This book is copyright protected. This book is only for personal use. You cannot amend, distribute, sell, use, quote, or paraphrase any part, or the content within this book, without the consent of the author or publisher.

Disclaimer Notice:

Please note the information contained within this document is for educational and entertainment purposes only. All effort has been executed to present accurate, up-to-date, and reliable, complete information. No warranties of any kind are declared or implied. Readers acknowledge that the author is not engaging in the rendering of legal, financial, medical, or professional advice. The content within this book has been derived from various sources. Please consult a licensed professional before attempting any techniques outlined in this book.

By reading this document, the reader agrees that under no circumstances is the author responsible for any losses, direct or indirect, which are incurred as a result of the use of the information contained within this document, including, but not limited to, — errors, omissions, or inaccuracies.

Table of Contents

Breakfast Recipes 1

Classic Spanish Tortilla With Tuna 2

Creamy Peach Smoothie 3

Artichoke Omelet With Goat Cheese 4

Hot Zucchini & Egg Nests 5

Granola & Berry Parfait 6

Zucchini & Tomato Cheese Tart 7

Falafel Balls With Tahini Sauce 9

Mushroom & Zucchini Egg Muffins 11

Spinach And Egg Breakfast Wraps 12

Easy Zucchini & Egg Stuffed Tomatoes..................... 14

Kale-proscuitto Porridge... 15

Cream Peach Smoothie 16

Classic Socca 17

Raspberry-yogurt Smoothie 18

Lime Watermelon Yogurt Smoothie 19

Maple Berry & Walnut Oatmeal.................................. 20

Fish And Seafood 21

Saucy Cod With Calamari Rings 22

Cheesy Smoked Salmon Crostini 23

Spiced Citrus Sole 24

Roasted Trout Stuffed With Veggies 25

Garlic Shrimp With Arugula Pesto 27

Juicy Basil-tomato Scallops 29

Asian-inspired Tuna Lettuce Wraps 30

Baked Halibut With Eggplants 31

Shrimp Quinoa Bowl With Black Olives 32

White Wine Cod Fillets 33

Sicilian-style Squid With Zucchini 34

Oven-baked Spanish Salmon 35

Lemon Shrimp With Black Olives 36

Mediterranean Grilled Sea Bass 37

Lemon-parsley Swordfish 39

Parsley Halibut With Roasted Peppers 40

Tuna And Zucchini Patties 42

Lemon Cioppino 44

Vegetable Mains And Meatless Recipes 46

Sweet Potato Chickpea Buddha Bowl 47

Roasted Vegetable Medley 49

Simple Honey-glazed Baby Carrots 51

Steamed Beetroot With Nutty Yogurt 52

Tomatoes Filled With Tabbouleh 53

Parsley & Olive Zucchini Bake 55

Chili Vegetable Skillet 56

Grilled Vegetable Skewers 58

Spicy Potato Wedges 59

Minty Broccoli & Walnuts 60

Balsamic Grilled Vegetables 61

Beans , Grains, And Pastas 62

Cherry, Apricot, And Pecan Brown Rice Bowl 63

Broccoli And Carrot Pasta Salad 65

Lemony Tuna Barley With Capers 66

Brown Rice Pilaf With Pistachios And Raisins....................... 67

Simple Lentil Risotto 69

Herb Bean Stew 70

Arroz Con Pollo 71

Quick Pesto Pasta 73

Lentil And Mushroom Pasta 74

Spinach Farfalle With Ricotta Cheese 76

Bell Pepper & Bean Salad 77

Spinach Lentils 78

Curry Apple Couscous With Leeks And Pecans 80

Basic Brown Rice Pilaf With Capers 81

Marrakech-style Couscous 82

Kale Chicken With Pappardelle 83

Mashed Beans With Cumin 85

Mustard Vegetable Millet... 87

Caprese Pasta With Roasted Asparagus 89

Rice And Blueberry Stuffed Sweet Potatoes 91

Garlic And Parsley Chickpeas.. 92

Quinoa & Watercress Salad With Nuts 94

Baked Rolled Oat With Pears And Pecans 95

Autumn Vegetable & Rigatoni Bake 97

Simple Green Rice.. 98

Poultry And Meats 100

Sautéed Ground Turkey With Brown Rice 101

Beef & Bell Pepper Bake 103

Pork & Vegetable Gratin 104

Dragon Pork Chops With Pickle Topping 105

Roasted Pork Tenderloin With Apple Sauce 106

Chicken Balls With Yogurt-cucumber Sauce 108

Crispy Pesto Chicken 110

Panko Grilled Chicken Patties 112

Greek-style Chicken & Egg Bake 113

Chicken Thighs With Roasted Artichokes 114

Parsley-dijon Chicken And Potatoes 116

Rosemary Fennel In Cherry Tomato Sauce 118

Thyme Zucchini & Chicken Stir-fry 120

Easy Grilled Pork Chops...121

Ground Beef, Tomato, And Kidney Bean Chili 122

Lamb Tagine With Couscous And Almonds 123

Catalan Chicken In Romesco Sauce.....................................125

Portuguese-style Chicken Breasts...127

Spicy Mustard Pork Tenderloin 128

Picante Beef Stew 129

Coriander Pork Roast 130

Saucy Turkey With Ricotta Cheese.......................................131

Peppery Chicken Bake..132

Fennel Beef Ribs..133

Milky Pork Stew..134

Grilled Beef With Mint-jalapeño Vinaigrette 135

Beef & Vegetable Stew 136

Almond-crusted Chicken Tenders With Honey 137

Pork Chops In Wine Sauce 139

Fruits, Desserts And Snacks 140

Avocado & Salmon Stuffed Cucumbers.. 141

Poached Pears In Red Wine.. 142

The Best Trail Mix 143

Strawberry Parfait 144

Greek Yogurt Affogato With Pistachios 145

Balsamic Squash Wedges With Walnuts 146

Turkish Baklava.. 147

Simple Peanut Butter And Chocolate Balls..................................... 149

Easy Blueberry And Oat Crisp 150

Roasted Eggplant Hummus 152

Turkish Dolma (stuffed Grape Leaves) 153

Chili Grilled Eggplant Rounds 154

Vegetarian Spinach-olive Pizza 155

Spicy Roasted Chickpeas 157

Speedy Granita 159

Cantaloupe & Watermelon Balls 160

Charred Asparagus 161

Breakfast Recipes

Classic Spanish Tortilla With Tuna

Servings:4

Cooking Time:30 Minutes

Ingredients:

- 7 oz canned tuna packed in water, flaked
- 2 plum tomatoes, seeded and diced
- 2 tbsp olive oil
- 6 large eggs, beaten
- 2 small potatoes, diced
- 2 green onions, chopped
- 1 roasted red bell pepper, sliced
- 1 tsp dried tarragon

Directions:

1. Preheat your broiler to high. Heat the olive oil in a skillet over medium heat. Fry the potatoes for 7 minutes until slightly soft. Add the green onions and cook for 3 minutes. Stir in the tuna, tomatoes, peppers, tarragon, and eggs. Cook for 8-10 minutes until the eggs are bubbling from the bottom and the bottom is slightly brown. Place the skillet under the preheated broiler for 5-6 minutes or until the middle is set and the top is slightly brown. Serve sliced into wedges.

Nutrition Info:

Per Serving: Calories: 422;Fat: 21g;Protein: 14g;Carbs: 46g.

Creamy Peach Smoothie

Servings:2

CookingTime: 0 Minutes

Ingredients:

- 2 cups packed frozen peaches, partially thawed
- ½ ripe avocado
- ½ cup plain or vanilla Greek yogurt
- 2 tablespoons flax meal
- 1 tablespoon honey
- 1 teaspoon orange extract
- 1 teaspoon vanilla extract

Directions:

1. Place all the ingredients in a blender and blend until completely mixed and smooth.
2. Divide the mixture into two bowls and serve immediately.

Nutrition Info:

Per Serving: Calories: 212;Fat: 13.1g;Protein: 6.0g;Carbs: 22.5g.

Artichoke Omelet With Goat Cheese

Servings:2

Cooking Time:20 Minutes

Ingredients:

- 1 cup canned artichoke hearts, chopped
- 1 tsp butter
- 4 eggs
- Salt and black pepper to taste
- 2 small tomato, chopped
- 4 oz goat cheese, crumbled

Directions:

1. Whisk the eggs with salt and pepper in a bowl. Melt butter in a skillet over medium heat and pour in the eggs, swirling the skillet until the base is golden, 4 minutes. Add the tomato, artichoke, and goat cheese and fold over the omelet. Serve.

Nutrition Info:

Per Serving: Calories: 310;Fat: 20g;Protein: 23g;Carbs: 16g.

Hot Zucchini & Egg Nests

Servings:4

Cooking Time:25 Minutes

Ingredients:

- 2 tbsp olive oil
- 4 eggs
- 1 lb zucchinis, shredded
- Salt and black pepper to taste
- ½ red chili pepper, minced
- 2 tbsp parsley, chopped

Directions:

1. Preheat the oven to 360 F. Combine zucchini, salt, pepper, and olive oil in a bowl. Form nest shapes with a spoon onto a greased baking sheet. Crack an egg into each nest and season with salt, pepper, and chili pepper. Bake for 11 minutes. Serve topped with parsley.

Nutrition Info:

Per Serving: Calories: 141;Fat: 11.6g;Protein: 7g;Carbs: 4.2g.

Granola & Berry Parfait

Servings:2

Cooking Time:5 Minutes

Ingredients:

- 2 cups berries
- 1 ½ cups Greek yogurt
- 1 tbsp powdered sugar
- ¼ cup granola

Directions:

1. Divide between two bowls a layer of berries, yogurt, and powdered sugar. Scatter with granola and serve.

Nutrition Info:

Per Serving: Calories: 244;Fat: 11g;Protein: 21g;Carbs: 43g.

Zucchini & Tomato Cheese Tart

Servings:6

Cooking Time:60 Minutes

Ingredients:

- 3 tbsp olive oil
- 5 sun-dried tomatoes, chopped
- 1 prepared pie crust
- 1 onion, chopped
- 2 garlic cloves, minced
- 2 zucchinis, chopped
- 1 red bell pepper, chopped
- 6 Kalamata olives, sliced
- 1 tsp fresh dill, chopped
- ½ cup Greek yogurt
- 1 cup feta cheese, crumbled
- 4 eggs
- 1 ½ cups milk
- Salt and black pepper to taste

Directions:

1. Preheat the oven to 380 F. Warm the olive oil in a skillet over medium heat and sauté garlic and onion for 3 minutes. Add in bell pepper and zucchini and sauté for another 3 minutes. Stir in olives, dill, salt, and pepper for 1-2 minutes and add tomatoes and feta cheese. Mix well and turn the heat off.

2. Press the crust gently into a lightly greased pie dish and prick it with a fork. Bake in the oven for 10-15 minutes until

pale gold. Spread the zucchini mixture over the pie crust. Whisk the eggs with salt, pepper, milk, and yogurt in a bowl, then pour over the zucchini layer. Bake for 25-30 minutes until golden brown. Let cool before serving.

Nutrition Info:

Per Serving: Calories: 220;Fat: 16g;Protein: 10g;Carbs: 14g.

Falafel Balls With Tahini Sauce

Servings:4

Cooking Time: 20 Minutes

Ingredients:

- Tahini Sauce:
- ½ cup tahini
- 2 tablespoons lemon juice
- ¼ cup finely chopped flat-leaf parsley
- 2 cloves garlic, minced
- ½ cup cold water, as needed
- Falafel:
- 1 cup dried chickpeas, soaked overnight, drained
- ¼ cup chopped flat-leaf parsley
- ¼ cup chopped cilantro
- 1 large onion, chopped
- 1 teaspoon cumin
- ½ teaspoon chili flakes
- 4 cloves garlic
- 1 teaspoon sea salt
- 5 tablespoons almond flour
- 1½ teaspoons baking soda, dissolved in 1 teaspoon water
- 2 cups peanut oil
- 1 medium bell pepper, chopped
- 1 medium tomato, chopped
- 4 whole-wheat pita breads

Directions:

1. Make the Tahini Sauce:
2. Combine the ingredients for the tahini sauce in a small bowl. Stir to mix well until smooth.

3. Wrap the bowl in plastic and refrigerate until ready to serve.
4. Make the Falafel:
5. Put the chickpeas, parsley, cilantro, onion, cumin, chili flakes, garlic, and salt in a food processor. Pulse to mix well but not puréed.
6. Add the flour and baking soda to the food processor, then pulse to form a smooth and tight dough.
7. Put the dough in a large bowl and wrap in plastic. Refrigerate for at least 2 hours to let it rise.
8. Divide and shape the dough into walnut-sized small balls.
9. Pour the peanut oil in a large pot and heat over high heat until the temperature of the oil reaches 375ºF.
10. Drop 6 balls into the oil each time, and fry for 5 minutes or until golden brown and crispy. Turn the balls with a strainer to make them fried evenly.
11. Transfer the balls on paper towels with the strainer, then drain the oil from the balls.
12. Roast the pita breads in the oven for 5 minutes or until golden brown, if needed, then stuff the pitas with falafel balls and top with bell peppers and tomatoes. Drizzle with tahini sauce and serve immediately.

Nutrition Info:

Per Serving: Calories: 574;Fat: 27.1g;Protein: 19.8g;Carbs: 69.7g.

Mushroom & Zucchini Egg Muffins

Servings:4

Cooking Time:20 Minutes

Ingredients:

- 2 tbsp olive oil
- 1 cup Parmesan, grated
- 1 onion, chopped
- 1 cup mushrooms, sliced
- 1 red bell pepper, chopped
- 1 zucchini, chopped
- Salt and black pepper to taste
- 8 eggs, whisked
- 2 tbsp chives, chopped

Directions:

1. Preheat the oven to 360 F. Warm the olive oil in a skillet over medium heat and sauté onion, bell pepper, zucchini, mushrooms, salt, and pepper for 5 minutes until tender. Mix with eggs and season with salt and pepper. Distribute the mixture across muffin cups and top with the Parmesan cheese. Sprinkle with chives and bake for 10 minutes. Serve.

Nutrition Info:

Per Serving: Calories: 60;Fat: 4g;Protein: 5g;Carbs: 4g.

Spinach And Egg Breakfast Wraps

Servings:2

Cooking Time: 7 Minutes

Ingredients:

- 1 tablespoon olive oil
- ¼ cup minced onion
- 3 to 4 tablespoons minced sun-dried tomatoes in olive oil and herbs
- 3 large eggs, whisked
- 1½ cups packed baby spinach
- 1 ounce crumbled feta cheese
- Salt, to taste
- 2 whole-wheat tortillas

Directions:

1. Heat the olive oil in a large skillet over medium-high heat.
2. Sauté the onion and tomatoes for about 3 minutes, stirring occasionally, until softened.
3. Reduce the heat to medium. Add the whisked eggs and stir-fry for 1 to 2 minutes.
4. Stir in the baby spinach and scatter with the crumbled feta cheese. Season as needed with salt.
5. Remove the egg mixture from the heat to a plate. Set aside.
6. Working in batches, place 2 tortillas on a microwave-safe dish and microwave for about 20 seconds to make them warm.
7. Spoon half of the egg mixture into each tortilla. Fold them in half and roll up, then serve.

Nutrition Info:

Per Serving: Calories: 434;Fat: 28.1g;Protein: 17.2g;Carbs: 30.8g.

Easy Zucchini & Egg Stuffed Tomatoes

Servings:4

Cooking Time:40 Minutes

Ingredients:

- 1 tbsp olive oil
- 1 small zucchini, grated
- 8 tomatoes, insides scooped
- 8 eggs
- Salt and black pepper to taste

Directions:

1. Preheat the oven to 360 F. Place tomatoes on a greased baking dish. Mix the zucchini with olive oil, salt, and pepper. Divide the mixture between the tomatoes and crack an egg on each one. Bake for 20-25 minutes. Serve warm.

Nutrition Info:

Per Serving: Calories: 280;Fat: 22g;Protein: 14g;Carbs: 12g.

Kale-proscuitto Porridge

Servings:2

Cooking Time:30 Minutes

Ingredients:

- 1 tbsp olive oil
- 1 green onion, chopped
- 1 oz prosciutto, chopped
- 2 cups kale
- ¾ cup old-fashioned oats
- 2 tbsp Parmesan, grated
- Salt and black pepper to taste

Directions:

1. Warm the olive oil in a pan over medium heat. Sauté the onion and prosciutto and sauté for 4 minutes or until the prosciutto is crisp and the onion turns golden. Add the kale and stir for 5 minutes until wilted. Transfer to a bowl.
2. Add the oats to the pan and let them toast for 2 minutes. Add 1 ½ of water or chicken stock and bring to a boil. Reduce the heat to low, cover, and let the oats simmer for 10 minutes or until the liquid is absorbed and the oats are tender.
3. Stir in Parmesan cheese, and add the onions, prosciutto, and kale back to the pan and cook until creamy but not dry. Adjust the seasoning with salt and pepper and serve.

Nutrition Info:

Per Serving: Calories: 258;Fat: 12g;Protein: 11g;Carbs: 29g.

Cream Peach Smoothie

Servings:1

Cooking Time:5 Minutes

Ingredients:

- 1 large peach, sliced
- 6 oz peach Greek yogurt
- 2 tbsp almond milk
- 2 ice cubes

Directions:

1. Blend the peach, yogurt, almond milk, and ice cubes in your food processor until thick and creamy. Serve and enjoy!

Nutrition Info:

Per Serving: Calories: 228;Fat: 3g;Protein: 11g;Carbs: 41.6g.

Classic Socca

Servings:4

Cooking Time: 10 Minutes

Ingredients:

- 1½ cups chickpea flour
- ½ teaspoon ground turmeric
- ½ teaspoon sea salt
- ½ teaspoon ground black pepper
- 2 tablespoons plus 2 teaspoons extra-virgin olive oil
- 1½ cups water

Directions:

1. Combine the chickpea flour, turmeric, salt, and black pepper in a bowl. Stir to mix well, then gently mix in 2 tablespoons of olive oil and water. Stir to mix until smooth.
2. Heat 2 teaspoons of olive oil in an 8-inch nonstick skillet over medium-high heat until shimmering.
3. Add half cup of the mixture into the skillet and swirl the skillet so the mixture coat the bottom evenly.
4. Cook for 5 minutes or until lightly browned and crispy. Flip the socca halfway through the cooking time. Repeat with the remaining mixture.
5. Slice and serve warm.

Nutrition Info:

Per Serving: Calories: 207;Fat: 10.2g;Protein: 7.9g;Carbs: 20.7g.

Raspberry-yogurt Smoothie

Servings:2

Cooking Time:10 Minutes

Ingredients:

- 2 cups raspberries
- 1 tsp honey
- 1 cup natural yogurt
- ½ cup milk
- 8 ice cubes

Directions:

1. In a food processor, combine yogurt, raspberries, honey, and milk. Blitz until smooth. Add in ice cubes and pulse until uniform. Serve right away.

Nutrition Info:

Per Serving: Calories: 187;Fat: 7g;Protein: 8g;Carbs: 26g.

Lime Watermelon Yogurt Smoothie

Servings:6

Cooking Time:5 Minutes

Ingredients:

- ½ cup almond milk
- 2 cups watermelon, cubed
- ½ cup Greek yogurt
- ½ tsp lime zest

Directions:

1. In a food processor, blend watermelon, almond milk, lime zest, and yogurt until smooth. Serve into glasses.

Nutrition Info:

Per Serving: Calories: 260;Fat: 10g;Protein: 2g;Carbs: 6g.

Maple Berry & Walnut Oatmeal

Servings:2

Cooking Time:10 Minutes

Ingredients:

- 1 cup mixed berries
- 1 ½ cups rolled oats
- 2 tbsp walnuts, chopped
- 2 tsp maple syrup

Directions:

1. Cook the oats according to the package instructions and share in 2 bowls. Microwave the maple syrup and berries for 30 seconds; stir well. Pour over each bowl. Top with walnuts.

Nutrition Info:

Per Serving: Calories: 262;Fat: 10g;Protein: 15g;Carbs: 57g.

Fish And Seafood

Saucy Cod With Calamari Rings

Servings:4

Cooking Time:20 Minutes

Ingredients:

- 1 lb cod, skinless and cubed
- 2 tbsp olive oil
- 1 mango, peeled and cubed
- ½ lb calamari rings
- 1 tbsp garlic chili sauce
- ¼ cup lime juice
- ½ tsp smoked paprika
- ½ tsp cumin, ground
- 2 garlic cloves, minced
- Salt and black pepper to taste

Directions:

1. Warm the olive oil in a skillet over medium heat and cook chili sauce, lime juice, paprika, cumin, garlic, salt, pepper, and mango for 3 minutes. Stir in cod and calamari and cook for another 7 minutes. Serve warm.

Nutrition Info:

Per Serving: Calories: 290;Fat: 13g;Protein: 16g;Carbs: 12g.

Cheesy Smoked Salmon Crostini

Servings:4

Cooking Time:10 Min + Chilling Time

Ingredients:

- 4 oz smoked salmon, sliced
- 2 oz feta cheese, crumbled
- 4 oz cream cheese, softened
- 2 tbsp horseradish sauce
- 2 tsp orange zest
- 1 red onion, chopped
- 2 tbsp chives, chopped
- 1 baguette, sliced and toasted

Directions:

1. In a bowl, mix cream cheese, horseradish sauce, onion, feta cheese, and orange zest until smooth. Spread the mixture on the baguette slices. Top with salmon and chives to serve.

Nutrition Info:

Per Serving: Calories: 290;Fat: 19g;Protein: 26g;Carbs: 5g.

Spiced Citrus Sole

Servings:4

Cooking Time: 10 Minutes

Ingredients:

- 1 teaspoon garlic powder
- 1 teaspoon chili powder
- ½ teaspoon lemon zest
- ½ teaspoon lime zest
- ¼ teaspoon smoked paprika
- ¼ teaspoon freshly ground black pepper
- Pinch sea salt
- 4 sole fillets, patted dry
- 1 tablespoon extra-virgin olive oil
- 2 teaspoons freshly squeezed lime juice

Directions:

2. Preheat the oven to 450ºF. Line a baking sheet with aluminum foil and set aside.
3. Mix together the garlic powder, chili powder, lemon zest, lime zest, paprika, pepper, and salt in a small bowl until well combined.
4. Arrange the sole fillets on the prepared baking sheet and rub the spice mixture all over the fillets until well coated. Drizzle the olive oil and lime juice over the fillets.
5. Bake in the preheated oven for about 8 minutes until flaky.
6. Remove from the heat to a plate and serve.

Nutrition Info:

Per Serving: Calories: 183;Fat: 5.0g;Protein: 32.1g;Carbs: 0g.

Roasted Trout Stuffed With Veggies

Servings:2

Cooking Time: 25 Minutes

Ingredients:

- 2 whole trout fillets, dressed (cleaned but with bones and skin intact)
- 1 tablespoon extra-virgin olive oil
- ¼ teaspoon salt
- ⅛ teaspoon freshly ground black pepper
- 1 small onion, thinly sliced
- ½ red bell pepper, seeded and thinly sliced
- 1 poblano pepper, seeded and thinly sliced
- 2 or 3 shiitake mushrooms, sliced
- 1 lemon, sliced
- Nonstick cooking spray

Directions:

1. Preheat the oven to 425ºF. Spray a baking sheet with nonstick cooking spray.
2. Rub both trout fillets, inside and out, with the olive oil. Season with salt and pepper.
3. Mix together the onion, bell pepper, poblano pepper, and mushrooms in a large bowl. Stuff half of this mixture into the cavity of each fillet. Top the mixture with 2 or 3 lemon slices inside each fillet.
4. Place the fish on the prepared baking sheet side by side. Roast in the preheated oven for 25 minutes, or until the fish is cooked through and the vegetables are tender.

5. Remove from the oven and serve on a plate.

Nutrition Info:

Per Serving: Calories: 453;Fat: 22.1g;Protein: 49.0g;Carbs: 13.8g.

Garlic Shrimp With Arugula Pesto

Servings:2

Cooking Time: 5 Minutes

Ingredients:

- 3 cups lightly packed arugula
- ½ cup lightly packed basil leaves
- ¼ cup walnuts
- 3 tablespoons olive oil
- 3 medium garlic cloves
- 2 tablespoons grated Parmesan cheese
- 1 tablespoon freshly squeezed lemon juice
- Salt and freshly ground black pepper, to taste
- 1 package zucchini noodles
- 8 ounces cooked, shelled shrimp
- 2 Roma tomatoes, diced

Directions:

1. Process the arugula, basil, walnuts, olive oil, garlic, Parmesan cheese, and lemon juice in a food processor until smooth, scraping down the sides as needed. Season with salt and pepper to taste.
2. Heat a skillet over medium heat. Add the pesto, zucchini noodles, and cooked shrimp. Toss to combine the sauce over the noodles and shrimp, and cook until heated through.
3. Taste and season with more salt and pepper as needed. Serve topped with the diced tomatoes.

Nutrition Info:

Per Serving: Calories: 435;Fat: 30.2g;Protein: 33.0g;Carbs: 15.1g.

Juicy Basil-tomato Scallops

Servings:4

Cooking Time:20 Minutes

Ingredients:

- 2 tbsp olive oil
- 1 tbsp basil, chopped
- 1 lb scallops, scrubbed
- 1 tbsp garlic, minced
- 1 onion, chopped
- 6 tomatoes, cubed
- 1 cup heavy cream
- 1 tbsp parsley, chopped

Directions:

1. Warm the olive oil in a skillet over medium heat and cook garlic and onion for 2 minutes. Stir in scallops, basil, tomatoes, heavy cream, and parsley and cook for an additional 7 minutes. Serve immediately.

Nutrition Info:

Per Serving: Calories: 270;Fat: 12g;Protein: 11g;Carbs: 17g.

Asian-inspired Tuna Lettuce Wraps

Servings:2

Cooking Time: 0 Minutes

Ingredients:

- ⅓ cup almond butter
- 1 tablespoon freshly squeezed lemon juice
- 1 teaspoon low-sodium soy sauce
- teaspoon curry powder
- ½ teaspoon sriracha, or to taste
- ½ cup canned water chestnuts, drained and chopped
- 2 package tuna packed in water, drained
- 2 large butter lettuce leaves

Directions:

1. Stir together the almond butter, lemon juice, soy sauce, curry powder, sriracha in a medium bowl until well mixed. Add the water chestnuts and tuna and stir until well incorporated.

2. Place 2 butter lettuce leaves on a flat work surface, spoon half of the tuna mixture onto each leaf and roll up into a wrap. Serve immediately.

Nutrition Info:

Per Serving: Calories: 270;Fat: 13.9g;Protein: 19.1g;Carbs: 18.5g.

Baked Halibut With Eggplants

Servings:4

Cooking Time:35 Minutes

Ingredients:

- 2 tbsp olive oil
- ¼ cup tomato sauce
- 4 halibut fillets, boneless
- 2 eggplants, sliced
- Salt and black pepper to taste
- 2 tbsp balsamic vinegar
- 2 tbsp chives, chopped

Directions:

- Preheat the oven to 380F. Warm the olive oil in a skillet over medium heat and fry the eggplant slices for 5-6 minutes, turning once; reserve. Add the tomato sauce, salt, pepper, and vinegar to the skillet and cook for 5 minutes. Return the eggplants to the skillet and cook for 2 minutes. Remove to a plate. Place the halibut fillets on a greased baking tray and bake for 12-15 minutes. Serve the halibut over the eggplants sprinkled with chives.

Nutrition Info:

Per Serving: Calories: 300;Fat: 13g;Protein: 16g;Carbs: 19g.

Shrimp Quinoa Bowl With Black Olives

Servings:4

Cooking Time:20 Minutes

Ingredients:

- 10 black olives, pitted and halved
- ¼ cup olive oil
- 1 cup quinoa
- 1 lemon, cut in wedges
- 1 lb shrimp, peeled and cooked
- 3 tomatoes, sliced
- 2 bell peppers, thinly sliced
- 1 red onion, chopped
- 1 tsp dried dill
- 1 tbsp fresh parsley, chopped
- Salt and black pepper to taste

Directions:

- Place the quinoa in a pot and cover with 2 cups of water over medium heat. Bring to a boil, reduce the heat, and simmer for 12-15 minutes or until tender. Remove from heat and fluff it with a fork. Mix in the quinoa with olive oil, dill, parsley, salt, and black pepper. Stir in tomatoes, bell peppers, olives, and onion. Serve decorated with shrimp and lemon wedges.

Nutrition Info:

Per Serving: Calories: 662;Fat: 21g;Protein: 79g;Carbs: 38g.

White Wine Cod Fillets

Servings:4

Cooking Time:40 Minutes

Ingredients:

- 4 cod fillets
- Salt and black pepper to taste
- ½ fennel seeds, ground
- 1 tbsp olive oil
- ½ cup dry white wine
- ½ cup vegetable stock
- 2 garlic cloves, minced
- 1 tsp chopped fresh sage
- 4 rosemary sprigs

Directions:

1. Preheat oven to 375 F. Season the cod fillets with salt, pepper, and ground fennel seeds and place them in a greased baking dish. Add the wine, stock, garlic, and sage and drizzle with olive oil. Cover with foil and bake for 20 minutes until the fish flakes easily with a fork. Remove the fillets from the dish. Place the liquid in a saucepan over high heat and cook, stirring frequently, until reduced by half, about 10 minutes. Serve the fish topped with sauce and fresh rosemary sprigs.

Nutrition Info:

Per Serving: Calories: 89;Fat: 0.6g;Protein: 18g;Carbs: 1.8g.

Sicilian-style Squid With Zucchini

Servings:4

Cooking Time:25 Minutes

Ingredients:

- 2 tbsp olive oil
- 10 oz squid, cut into pieces
- 2 zucchinis, chopped
- 2 tbsp cilantro, chopped
- 1 jalapeno pepper, chopped
- 3 tbsp balsamic vinegar
- Salt and black pepper to taste
- 1 tbsp dill, chopped

Directions:

1. Warm the olive oil in a skillet over medium heat and sauté squid for 5 minutes. Stir in zucchini, cilantro, jalapeño pepper, vinegar, salt, pepper, and dill and cook for another 10 minutes. Serve right away.

Nutrition Info:

Per Serving: Calories: 240;Fat: 16g;Protein: 12g;Carbs: 24g.

Oven-baked Spanish Salmon

Servings:4

Cooking Time:30 Minutes

Ingredients:

- 15 green pimiento-stuffed olives
- 2 small red onions, sliced
- 1 cup fennel bulbs shaved
- 1 cup cherry tomatoes
- Salt and black pepper to taste
- 1 tsp cumin seeds
- ½ tsp smoked paprika
- 4 salmon fillets
- ½ cup chicken broth
- 3 tbsp olive oil
- 2 cups cooked farro

Directions:

1. Preheat oven to 375 F. In a bowl, combine the onions, fennel, tomatoes, and olives. Season with salt, pepper, cumin, and paprika and mix well. Spread out on a greased baking dish. Arrange the fish fillets over the vegetables, season with salt, and gently pour the broth over. Drizzle with olive oil and bake for 20 minutes. Serve over farro.

Nutrition Info:

Per Serving: Calories: 475;Fat: 18g;Protein: 50g;Carbs: 26g.

Lemon Shrimp With Black Olives

Servings:4

Cooking Time:25 Minutes

Ingredients:

- 1 lb shrimp, peeled and deveined
- 3 tbsp olive oil
- 1 lemon, juiced
- 1 tbsp flour
- 1 cup fish stock
- Salt and black pepper to taste
- 1 cup black olives, halved
- 1 tbsp rosemary, chopped

Directions:

1. Warm the olive oil in a skillet over medium heat and sear shrimp for 4 minutes on both sides; set aside. In the same skillet over low heat, stir in the flour for 2-3 minutes.
2. Gradually pour in the fish stock and lemon juice while stirring and simmer for 3-4 minutes until the sauce thickens. Adjust the seasoning with salt and pepper and mix in shrimp, olives, and rosemary. Serve immediately.

Nutrition Info:

Per Serving: Calories: 240;Fat: 16g;Protein: 9g;Carbs: 16g.

Mediterranean Grilled Sea Bass

Servings:6

Cooking Time: 20 Minutes

Ingredients:
- ¼ teaspoon onion powder
- ¼ teaspoon garlic powder
- ¼ teaspoon paprika
- Lemon pepper and sea salt to taste
- 2 pounds sea bass
- 3 tablespoons extra-virgin olive oil, divided
- 2 large cloves garlic, chopped
- 1 tablespoon chopped Italian flat leaf parsley

Directions:

1. Preheat the grill to high heat.

2. Place the onion powder, garlic powder, paprika, lemon pepper, and sea salt in a large bowl and stir to combine.

3. Dredge the fish in the spice mixture, turning until well coated.

4. Heat 2 tablespoon of olive oil in a small skillet. Add the garlic and parsley and cook for 1 to 2 minutes, stirring occasionally. Remove the skillet from the heat and set aside.

5. Brush the grill grates lightly with remaining 1 tablespoon olive oil.

6. Grill the fish for about 7 minutes. Flip the fish and drizzle with the garlic mixture and cook for an additional 7 minutes, or until the fish flakes when pressed lightly with a fork.

7. Serve hot.

Nutrition Info:

Per Serving: Calories: 200;Fat: 10.3g;Protein: 26.9g;Carbs: 0.6g.

Lemon-parsley Swordfish

Servings:4

Cooking Time: 17 To 20 Minutes

Ingredients:

- 1 cup fresh Italian parsley
- ¼ cup lemon juice
- ¼ cup extra-virgin olive oil
- ¼ cup fresh thyme
- 2 cloves garlic
- ½ teaspoon salt
- 4 swordfish steaks Olive oil spray

Directions:

1. Preheat the oven to 450ºF. Grease a large baking dish generously with olive oil spray.

2. Place the parsley, lemon juice, olive oil, thyme, garlic, and salt in a food processor and pulse until smoothly blended.

3. Arrange the swordfish steaks in the greased baking dish and spoon the parsley mixture over the top.

4. Bake in the preheated oven for 17 to 20 minutes until flaky.

5. Divide the fish among four plates and serve hot.

Nutrition Info:

Per Serving: Calories: 396;Fat: 21.7g;Protein: 44.2g;Carbs: 2.9g.

Parsley Halibut With Roasted Peppers

Servings:4

Cooking Time:45 Minutes

Ingredients:

- 3 tbsp olive oil
- 1 tsp butter
- 2 red peppers, cut into wedges
- 4 halibut fillets
- 2 shallots, cut into rings
- 2 garlic cloves, minced
- ¾ cup breadcrumbs
- 2 tbsp chopped fresh parsley
- Salt and black pepper to taste

Directions:

1. Preheat oven to 450 F. Combine red peppers, garlic, shallots, 1 tbsp of olive oil, salt, and pepper in a bowl. Spread on a baking sheet and bake for 40 minutes. Warm the remaining olive oil in a pan over medium heat and brown the breadcrumbs for 4-5 minutes, stirring constantly. Set aside.
2. Clean the pan and add in the butter to melt. Sprinkle the fish with salt and pepper. Add to the butter and cook for 8-10 minutes on both sides. Divide the pepper mixture between 4 plates and top with halibut fillets. Spread the crunchy breadcrumbs all over and top with parsley. Serve and enjoy!

Nutrition Info:

Per Serving: Calories: 511;Fat: 19.4g;Protein: 64g;Carbs: 18g.

Tuna And Zucchini Patties

Servings:4

Cooking Time: 12 Minutes

Ingredients:

- 3 slices whole-wheat sandwich bread, toasted
- 2 cans tuna in olive oil, drained
- 1 cup shredded zucchini
- 1 large egg, lightly beaten
- ¼ cup diced red bell pepper
- 1 tablespoon dried oregano
- 1 teaspoon lemon zest
- ¼ teaspoon freshly ground black pepper
- ¼ teaspoon kosher or sea salt
- 1 tablespoon extra-virgin olive oil
- Salad greens or 4 whole-wheat rolls, for serving (optional)

Directions:

1. Crumble the toast into bread crumbs with your fingers (or use a knife to cut into ¼-inch cubes) until you have 1 cup of loosely packed crumbs. Pour the crumbs into a large bowl. Add the tuna, zucchini, beaten egg, bell pepper, oregano, lemon zest, black pepper, and salt. Mix well with a fork. With your hands, form the mixture into four (½cup-size) patties. Place them on a plate, and press each patty flat to about ¾-inch thick.

2. In a large skillet over medium-high heat, heat the oil until it's very hot, about 2 minutes.

3. Add the patties to the hot oil, then reduce the heat down to medium. Cook the patties for 5 minutes, flip with a spatula, and cook for an additional 5 minutes. Serve the patties on salad greens or whole-wheat rolls, if desired.

Nutrition Info:

Per Serving: Calories: 757;Fat: 72.0g;Protein: 5.0g;Carbs: 26.0g.

Lemon Cioppino

Servings:6

Cooking Time:6 Minutes

Ingredients:

- 1 lb mussels, scrubbed, debearded
- 1 lb large shrimp, peeled and deveined
- 1 ½ lb haddock fillets, cut into chunks
- 3 tbsp olive oil
- 1 fennel bulb, thinly sliced
- 1 onion, chopped
- 3 large shallots, chopped
- Salt to taste
- 4 garlic cloves, minced
- ¼ tsp red pepper flakes
- ¼ cup tomato paste
- 1 can diced tomatoes
- 1 ½ cups dry white wine
- 5 cups vegetable stock
- 1 bay leaf
- 1 lb clams, scrubbed
- 2 tbsp basil, chopped

Directions:

1. Warm the olive oil in a large pot over medium heat. Sauté the fennel, onion, garlic, and shallots for 8-10 minutes until tender. Add the red pepper flakes and sauté for 2 minutes. Stir in the tomato paste, tomatoes with their juices, wine, stock, salt, and bay leaf. Cover and bring to a simmer. Lower

the heat to low and simmer for 30 minutes until the flavors blend.

2. Pour in the clams and mussels and cook for about 5 minutes. Add the shrimp and fish. Simmer gently until the fish and shrimp are just cooked through, 5 minutes. Discard any clams and mussels that refuse to open and bay leaf. Top with basil.

Nutrition Info:

Per Serving: Calories: 163;Fat: 4.1g;Protein: 22g;Carbs: 8.3g.

Vegetable Mains And Meatless Recipes

Sweet Potato Chickpea Buddha Bowl

Servings:2

Cooking Time: 10 To 15 Minutes

Ingredients:

- Sauce:
- 1 tablespoon tahini
- 2 tablespoons plain Greek yogurt
- 2 tablespoons hemp seeds
- 1 garlic clove, minced
- Pinch salt
- Freshly ground black pepper, to taste
- Bowl:
- 1 small sweet potato, peeled and finely diced
- 1 teaspoon extra-virgin olive oil
- 1 cup from 1 can low-sodium chickpeas, drained and rinsed
- 2 cups baby kale

Directions:

1. Make the Sauce

2. Whisk together the tahini and yogurt in a small bowl.

3. Stir in the hemp seeds and minced garlic. Season with salt pepper. Add 2 to 3 tablespoons water to create a creamy yet pourable consistency and set aside.

4. Make the Bowl

5. Preheat the oven to 425ºF. Line a baking sheet with parchment paper.

6. Place the sweet potato on the prepared baking sheet and drizzle with the olive oil. Toss well

7. Roast in the preheated oven for 10 to 15 minutes, stirring once during cooking, or until fork-tender and browned.

8. In each of 2 bowls, place ½ cup of chickpeas, 1 cup of baby kale, and half of the cooked sweet potato. Serve drizzled with half of the prepared sauce.

Nutrition Info:

Per Serving: Calories: 323;Fat: 14.1g;Protein: 17.0g;Carbs: 36.0g.

Roasted Vegetable Medley

Servings:2

Cooking Time:65 Minutes

Ingredients:

- 1 head garlic, cloves split apart, unpeeled
- 3 tbsp olive oil
- 2 carrots, cut into strips
- ¼ lb asparagus, chopped
- ½ lb Brussels sprouts, halved
- 2 cups broccoli florets
- 1 cup cherry tomatoes
- ½ fresh lemon, sliced
- Salt and black pepper to taste

Directions:

1. Preheat oven to 375 F. Drizzle the garlic cloves with some olive oil and lightly wrap them in a small piece of foil. Place the packet in the oven and roast for 30 minutes. Place all the vegetables and the lemon slices into a large mixing bowl. Drizzle with the remaining olive oil and season with salt and pepper. Increase the oven to 400 F. Pour the vegetables on a sheet pan in a single layer, leaving the packet of garlic cloves on the pan. Roast for 20 minutes, shaking occasionally until tender. Remove the pan from the oven. Let the garlic cloves sit until cool enough to handle, then remove the skins. Top the vegetables with roasted garlic and serve.

Nutrition Info:

Per Serving: Calories: 256;Fat: 15g;Protein: 7g;Carbs: 31g.

Simple Honey-glazed Baby Carrots

Servings:2

Cooking Time: 6 Minutes

Ingredients:

- ⅔ cup water
- 1½ pounds baby carrots
- 4 tablespoons almond butter
- ½ cup honey
- teaspoon dried thyme
- 1½ teaspoons dried dill
- Salt, to taste

Directions:

1. Pour the water into the Instant Pot and add a steamer basket. Place the baby carrots in the basket.
2. Secure the lid. Select the Manual mode and set the cooking time for 4 minutes at High Pressure.
3. Once cooking is complete, do a quick pressure release. Carefully open the lid.
4. Transfer the carrots to a plate and set aside.
5. Pour the water out of the Instant Pot and dry it.
6. Press the Sauté button on the Instant Pot and heat the almond butter.
7. Stir in the honey, thyme, and dill.
8. Return the carrots to the Instant Pot and stir until well coated. Sauté for another 1 minute.
9. Taste and season with salt as needed. Serve warm.

Nutrition Info:

Per Serving: Calories: 575;Fat: 23.5g;Protein: 2.8g;Carbs: 90.6g.

Steamed Beetroot With Nutty Yogurt

Servings:4

Cooking Time:30 Min + Chilling Time

Ingredients:

- ¼ cup extra virgin olive oil
- 1 lb beetroots, cut into wedges
- 1 cup Greek yogurt
- 3 spring onions, sliced
- 5 dill pickles, finely chopped
- 2 garlic cloves, minced
- 2 tbsp fresh parsley, chopped
- 1 oz mixed nuts, crushed
- Salt to taste

Directions:

1. In a pot over medium heat, insert a steamer basket and pour in 1 cup of water. Place in the beetroots and steam for 10-15 minutes until tender. Remove to a plate and let cool. In a bowl, combine the pickles, spring onions, garlic, salt, 3 tbsp of olive oil, Greek yogurt, and nuts and mix well. Spread the yogurt mixture on a serving plate and arrange the beetroot wedges on top. Drizzle with the remaining olive oil and top with parsley. Serve and enjoy!

Nutrition Info:

- Per Serving: Calories: 271;Fat: 18g;Protein: 9.6g;Carbs: 22g.

Tomatoes Filled With Tabbouleh

Servings:4

Cooking Time:25 Minutes

Ingredients:

- 3 tbsp olive oil, divided
- 8 medium tomatoes
- ½ cup water
- ½ cup bulgur wheat
- ½ cups minced parsley
- ⅓ cup minced fresh mint
- 2 scallions, chopped
- 1 tsp sumac
- Salt and black pepper to taste
- 1 lemon, zested

Directions:

1. Place the bulgur wheat and 2 cups of salted water in a pot and bring to a boil. Lower the heat and simmer for 10 minutes or until tender. Remove the pot from the heat and cover with a lid. Let it sit for 15 minutes.
2. Preheat the oven to 400 F. Slice off the top of each tomato and scoop out the pulp and seeds using a spoon into a sieve set over a bowl. Drain and discard any excess liquid; chop the remaining pulp and place it in a large mixing bowl. Add in parsley, mint, scallions, sumac, lemon zest, lemon juice, bulgur, pepper, and salt, and mix well.

3. Spoon the filling into the tomatoes and place the lids on top. Drizzle with olive oil and bake for 15-20 minutes until the tomatoes are tender. Serve and enjoy!

Nutrition Info:

Per Serving: Calories: 160;Fat: 7g;Protein: 5g;Carbs: 22g.

Parsley & Olive Zucchini Bake

Servings:6

Cooking Time:1 Hour 40 Minutes

Ingredients:

- 3 tbsp olive oil
- 1 can tomatoes, diced
- 2 lb zucchinis, sliced
- 1 onion, chopped
- Salt and black pepper to taste
- 3 garlic cloves, minced
- ¼ tsp dried oregano
- ¼ tsp red pepper flakes
- 10 Kalamata olives, chopped
- 2 tbsp fresh parsley, chopped

Directions:

1. Preheat oven to 325 F. Warm the olive oil in a saucepan over medium heat. Sauté zucchini for about 3 minutes per side; transfer to a bowl. Stir-fry the onion and salt in the same saucepan for 3-5 minutes, stirring occasionally until onion soft and lightly golden. Stir in garlic, oregano, and pepper flakes and cook until fragrant, about 30 seconds.
2. Add in olives, tomatoes, salt, and pepper, bring to a simmer, and cook for about 10 minutes, stirring occasionally. Return the zucchini, cover, and transfer the pot to the oven. Bake for 10-15 minutes. Sprinkle with parsley and serve.

Nutrition Info:

Per Serving: Calories: 164;Fat: 6g;Protein: 1.5g;Carbs: 7.7g.

Chili Vegetable Skillet

Servings:4

Cooking Time:30 Minutes

Ingredients:

- 1 cup condensed cream of mushroom soup
- 1 ½ lb eggplants, cut into chunks
- 1 cup cremini mushrooms, sliced
- 4 tbsp olive oil
- 1 carrot, thinly sliced
- 1 can tomatoes
- ½ cup red onion, thinly sliced
- 2 garlic cloves, minced
- 1 tsp fresh rosemary
- 1 tsp chili pepper
- Salt and black pepper to taste
- 2 tbsp parsley, chopped
- ¼ cup Parmesan cheese, grated

Directions:

1. Warm the olive oil in a skillet over medium heat. Add in the eggplant and cook until golden brown on all sides, about 5 minutes; set aside. Add in the carrot, onion, and mushrooms and sauté for 4 more minutes to the same skillet. Add in garlic, rosemary, and chili pepper. Cook for another 30-40 seconds. Add in 1 cup of water, cream of mushroom soup, and tomatoes. Bring to a boil and lower the heat; simmer covered for 5 minutes. Mix in sautéed eggplants and parsley and cook for 10 more minutes.

Sprinkle with salt and black pepper. Serve topped with Parmesan cheese.

Nutrition Info:

Per Serving: Calories: 261;Fat: 18.7g;Protein: 5g;Carbs: 23g.

Grilled Vegetable Skewers

Servings:4

Cooking Time: 10 Minutes

Ingredients:

- 4 medium red onions, peeled and sliced into 6 wedges
- 4 medium zucchini, cut into 1-inch-thick slices
- 2 beefsteak tomatoes, cut into quarters
- 4 red bell peppers, cut into 2-inch squares
- 2 orange bell peppers, cut into 2-inch squares
- 2 yellow bell peppers, cut into 2-inch squares
- 2 tablespoons plus 1 teaspoon olive oil, divided

SPECIAL EQUIPMENT:

- 4 wooden skewers, soaked in water for at least 30 minutes

Directions:

1. Preheat the grill to medium-high heat.
2. Skewer the vegetables by alternating between red onion, zucchini, tomatoes, and the different colored bell peppers. Brush them with 2 tablespoons of olive oil.
3. Oil the grill grates with 1 teaspoon of olive oil and grill the vegetable skewers for 5 minutes. Flip the skewers and grill for 5 minutes more, or until they are cooked to your liking.
4. Let the skewers cool for 5 minutes before serving.

Nutrition Info:

Per Serving: Calories: 115;Fat: 3.0g;Protein: 3.5g;Carbs: 18.7g.

Spicy Potato Wedges

Servings:4

Cooking Time:30 Minutes

Ingredients:

- 1 ½ lb potatoes, peeled and cut into wedges
- 3 tbsp olive oil
- 1 tbsp minced fresh rosemary
- 2 tsp chili powder
- 3 garlic cloves, minced
- Salt and black pepper to taste

Directions:

1. Preheat the oven to 370 F. Toss the wedges with olive oil, garlic, salt, and pepper. Spread out in a roasting sheet. Roast for 15-20 minutes until browned and crisp at the edges. Remove and sprinkle with chili powder and rosemary.

Nutrition Info:

Per Serving: Calories: 152;Fat: 7g;Protein: 2.5g;Carbs: 21g.

Minty Broccoli & Walnuts

Servings:2

Cooking Time:10 Minutes

Ingredients:

- 1 garlic clove, minced
- ½ cups walnuts, chopped
- 3 cups broccoli florets, steamed
- 1 tbsp mint, chopped
- ½ lemon, juiced
- Salt and black pepper to taste

Directions:

1. Mix walnuts, broccoli, garlic, mint, lemon juice, salt, and pepper in a bowl. Serve chilled.

Nutrition Info:

Per Serving: Calories: 210;Fat: 7g;Protein: 4g;Carbs: 9g.

Balsamic Grilled Vegetables

Servings:4

Cooking Time:20 Minutes

Ingredients:

- ¼ cup olive oil
- 4 carrots, cut in half
- 2 onions, quartered
- 1 zucchini, cut into rounds
- 1 eggplant, cut into rounds
- 1 red bell pepper, chopped
- Salt and black pepper to taste
- Balsamic vinegar to taste

Directions:

1. Heat your grill to medium-high. Brush the vegetables lightly with olive oil, and season with salt and pepper. Grill the vegetables for 3–4 minutes per side. Transfer to a serving dish and drizzle with balsamic vinegar. Serve and enjoy!

Nutrition Info:

Per Serving: Calories: 184;Fat: 14g;Protein: 2.1g;Carbs: 14g.

Beans , Grains, And Pastas

Cherry, Apricot, And Pecan Brown Rice Bowl

Servings:2

Cooking Time: 1 Hour 1 Minutes

Ingredients:

- 2 tablespoons olive oil
- 2 green onions, sliced
- ½ cup brown rice
- 1 cup low -sodium chicken stock
- 2 tablespoons dried cherries
- 4 dried apricots, chopped
- 2 tablespoons pecans, toasted and chopped
- Sea salt and freshly ground pepper, to taste

Directions:

2. Heat the olive oil in a medium saucepan over medium-high heat until shimmering.
3. Add the green onions and sauté for 1 minutes or until fragrant.
4. Add the rice. Stir to mix well, then pour in the chicken stock.
5. Bring to a boil. Reduce the heat to low. Cover and simmer for 50 minutes or until the brown rice is soft.
6. Add the cherries, apricots, and pecans, and simmer for 10 more minutes or until the fruits are tender.
7. Pour them in a large serving bowl. Fluff with a fork. Sprinkle with sea salt and freshly ground pepper. Serve immediately.

Nutrition Info:

Per Serving: Calories: 451;Fat: 25.9g;Protein: 8.2g;Carbs: 50.4g.

Broccoli And Carrot Pasta Salad

Ingredients:

- 8 ounces whole-wheat pasta
- 2 cups broccoli florets
- 1 cup peeled and shredded carrots
- ¼ cup plain Greek yogurt
- Juice of 1 lemon
- 1 teaspoon red pepper flakes
- Sea salt and freshly ground pepper, to taste

Directions:

1. Bring a large pot of lightly salted water to a boil. Add the pasta to the boiling water and cook until al dente. Drain and let rest for a few minutes.
2. When cooled, combine the pasta with the veggies, yogurt, lemon juice, and red pepper flakes in a large bowl, and stir thoroughly to combine.
3. Taste and season to taste with salt and pepper. Serve immediately.

Nutrition Info:

Per Serving: Calories: 428;Fat: 2.9g;Protein: 15.9g;Carbs: 84.6g.

Lemony Tuna Barley With Capers

Servings:4

Cooking Time:50 Minutes

Ingredients:

- 2 tbsp olive oil
- 3 cups chicken stock
- 10 oz canned tuna, flaked
- 1 cup barley
- Salt and black pepper to taste
- 12 cherry tomatoes, halved
- ½ cup pepperoncini, sliced
- ¼ cup capers, drained
- ½ lemon, juiced

Directions:

1. Boil chicken stock in a saucepan over medium heat and add in barley. Cook covered for 40 minutes. Fluff the barley and remove to a bowl. Stir in tuna, salt, pepper, tomatoes, pepperoncini, olive oil, capers, and lemon juice. Serve.

Nutrition Info:

Per Serving: Calories: 260;Fat: 12g;Protein: 24g;Carbs: 17g.

Brown Rice Pilaf With Pistachios And Raisins

Servings:6

Cooking Time: 15 Minutes

Ingredients:

- 1 tablespoon extra-virgin olive oil
- 1 cup chopped onion
- ½ cup shredded carrot
- ½ teaspoon ground cinnamon
- 1 teaspoon ground cumin
- 2 cups brown rice
- 1¾ cups pure orange juice
- ¼ cup water
- ½ cup shelled pistachios
- 1 cup golden raisins
- ½ cup chopped fresh chives

Directions:

1. Heat the olive oil in a saucepan over medium-high heat until shimmering.
2. Add the onion and sauté for 5 minutes or until translucent.
3. Add the carrots, cinnamon, and cumin, then sauté for 1 minutes or until aromatic.
4. Pour int the brown rice, orange juice, and water. Bring to a boil. Reduce the heat to medium-low and simmer for 7 minutes or until the liquid is almost absorbed.

5. Transfer the rice mixture in a large serving bowl, then spread with pistachios, raisins, and chives. Serve immediately.

Nutrition Info:

Per Serving: Calories: 264;Fat: 7.1g;Protein: 5.2g;Carbs: 48.9g.

Simple Lentil Risotto

Servings:2

Cooking Time: 20 Minutes

Ingredients:

- ½ tablespoon olive oil
- ½ medium onion, chopped
- ½ cup dry lentils, soaked overnight
- ½ celery stalk, chopped
- sprig parsley, chopped
- ½ cup Arborio (short-grain Italian) rice
- 1 garlic clove, lightly mashed
- 2 cups vegetable stock

Directions:

1. Press the Sauté button to heat your Instant Pot.
2. Add the oil and onion to the Instant Pot and sauté for 5 minutes.
3. Add all the remaining ingredients to the Instant Pot.
4. Secure the lid. Select the Manual mode and set the cooking time for 15 minutes at High Pressure.
5. Once cooking is complete, do a natural pressure release for 20 minutes, then release any remaining pressure. Carefully open the lid.
6. Stir and serve hot.

Nutrition Info:

Per Serving: Calories: 261;Fat: 3.6g;Protein: 10.6g;Carbs: 47.1g.

Herb Bean Stew

Servings:4

Cooking Time:70 Minutes

Ingredients:
- 2 tbsp olive oil
- 3 tomatoes, cubed
- 1 yellow onion, chopped
- 1 celery stalk, chopped
- 2 tbsp parsley, chopped
- 2 garlic cloves, minced
- 1 cup lima beans, soaked
- 1 tsp paprika
- 1 tsp dried oregano
- ½ tsp dried thyme
- Salt and black pepper to taste

Directions:
1. Cover the lima beans with water in a pot and place over medium heat. Bring to a boil and cook for 30 minutes. Drain and set aside. Warm olive oil in the pot over medium heat and cook onion and garlic for 3 minutes. Stir in tomatoes, celery, oregano, thyme, and paprika and cook for 5 minutes. Pour in 3 cups of water and return the lima beans; season with salt and pepper. Simmer for 30 minutes. Top with parsley.

Nutrition Info:

Per Serving: Calories: 310;Fat: 16g;Protein: 16g;Carbs: 30g.

Arroz Con Pollo

Servings:4

Cooking Time:50 Minutes

Ingredients:

- 2 tbsp olive oil
- 1 lb chicken thighs, skinless
- 1 cup Spanish rice
- 2 cups chicken broth
- ½ cup spring onions, chopped
- ½ red bell pepper, chopped
- ¼ cup tomato paste
- 2 garlic cloves, minced
- ¼ cup white wine
- ½ tsp sweet paprika
- ¼ tsp turmeric
- ½ tsp dried basil
- ½ tsp dried tarragon
- Salt and black pepper to taste

Directions:

1. Warm the olive oil in a saucepan over medium heat and stir-fry the chicken for 8-10 minutes. Remove to a plate to cool. Add spring onions, bell pepper, and garlic to the saucepan and cook for 3 minutes. Pour in white wine to scrape off any bits from the bottom. Discard the bones from the chicken and shred it with a fork. Return to the saucepan and sprinkle with salt, black pepper, paprika, turmeric, tarragon, and basil. Stir in the rice, tomato paste,

and chicken broth. Cook covered for about 20 minutes. Serve and enjoy!

Nutrition Info:

Per Serving: Calories: 502;Fat: 17g;Protein: 39g;Carbs: 44g.

Quick Pesto Pasta

Servings:4

Cooking Time:20 Minutes

Ingredients:

- 1 lb linguine
- 2 tomatoes, chopped
- 10 oz basil pesto
- ½ cup pine nuts, toasted
- ½ cup Parmesan cheese, grated
- 1 lemon, zested

Directions:

1. Bring to a boil salted water in a pot over high heat. Add the linguine and cook according to package directions, 9-11 minutes. Drain and transfer to a serving bowl. Add the tomatoes, pesto, and lemon zest toss gently to coat the pasta. Sprinkle with Parmesan cheese and pine nuts and serve.

Nutrition Info:

Per Serving: Calories: 617;Fat: 17g;Protein: 23g;Carbs: 94g.

Lentil And Mushroom Pasta

Servings:2

Cooking Time: 50 Minutes

Ingredients:

- 2 tablespoons olive oil
- 1 large yellow onion, finely diced
- 2 portobello mushrooms, trimmed and chopped finely
- 2 tablespoons tomato paste
- 3 garlic cloves, chopped
- 1 teaspoon oregano
- 2½ cups water
- 1 cup brown lentils
- 1 can diced tomatoes with basil (with juice if diced)
- 1 tablespoon balsamic vinegar
- 8 ounces pasta of choice, cooked
- Salt and black pepper, to taste
- Chopped basil, for garnish

Directions:

1. Place a large stockpot over medium heat. Add the oil. Once the oil is hot, add the onion and mushrooms. Cover and cook until both are soft, about 5 minutes. Add the tomato paste, garlic, and oregano and cook 2 minutes, stirring constantly.
2. Stir in the water and lentils. Bring to a boil, then reduce the heat to medium-low and cook for 5 minutes, covered.

3. Add the tomatoes (and juice if using diced) and vinegar. Replace the lid, reduce the heat to low and cook until the lentils are tender, about 30 minutes.

4. Remove the sauce from the heat and season with salt and pepper to taste. Garnish with the basil and serve over the cooked pasta.

Nutrition Info:

Per Serving: Calories: 463;Fat: 15.9g;Protein: 12.5g;Carbs: 70.8g.

Spinach Farfalle With Ricotta Cheese

Servings:4

Cooking Time:25 Minutes

Ingredients:

- ¼ cup extra-virgin olive oil
- ½ cup crumbled ricotta cheese
- 2 tbsp black olives, halved
- 4 cups fresh baby spinach, chopped
- 2 tbsp scallions, chopped
- 16 oz farfalle pasta
- ¼ cup red wine vinegar
- 2 tsp lemon juice
- Salt and black pepper to taste

Directions:

1. Cook the farfalle pasta to pack instructions, drain and let it to cool. Mix the scallions, spinach, and cooled pasta in a bowl. Top with ricotta and olives. Combine the vinegar, olive oil, lemon juice, salt, and pepper in another bowl. Pour over the pasta mixture and toss to combine. Serve chilled.

Nutrition Info:

Per Serving: Calories: 377;Fat: 16g;Protein: 12g;Carbs: 44g.

Bell Pepper & Bean Salad

Servings:6

Cooking Time:30 Minutes

Ingredients:

- ¼ cup extra-virgin olive oil
- 3 garlic cloves, minced
- 2 cans cannellini beans
- Salt and black pepper to taste
- 2 tsp sherry vinegar
- 1 red onion, sliced
- 1 red bell pepper, chopped
- ¼ cup chopped fresh parsley
- 2 tsp chopped fresh chives
- ¼ tsp crushed red pepper

Directions:

1. Warm 1 tbsp of olive oil in a saucepan over medium heat. Sauté the garlic until it turns golden but not brown, about 3 minutes. Add beans, 2 cups of water, and salt, and pepper, and bring to a simmer. Heat off. Let sit for 20 minutes.
2. Mix well the vinegar and red onion in a salad bowl. Drain the beans and remove the garlic. Add beans, remaining olive oil, bell pepper, parsley, crushed red pepper, chives, salt, and pepper to the onion mixture and gently toss to combine.

Nutrition Info:

Per Serving: Calories: 131;Fat: 7.7g;Protein: 6g;Carbs: 13.5g.

Spinach Lentils

Servings:6

Cooking Time:30 Minutes

Ingredients:

- 2 tbsp olive oil
- 4 garlic cloves, sliced thin
- Salt and black pepper to taste
- 1 onion, chopped
- 1 tsp ground coriander
- 1 tsp dried thyme
- 1 tsp ground cumin
- 1 cup lentils, rinsed
- 8 oz spinach, chopped

Directions:

1. Warm the olive oil in a pot over medium heat. Sauté the garlic for 2-3 minutes, stirring often, until crisp and golden but not brown. Remove the garlic to a paper towel–lined plate and season lightly with salt; set aside. Add the onion to the pot and cook for 3 minutes until softened and lightly browned. Stir in salt, thyme, coriander, and cumin for 1 minute until fragrant.

2. Pour in 2 ½ cups of water and lentils and bring to a simmer. Lower the heat to low, cover, and simmer gently, stirring occasionally for 15 minutes until lentils are mostly tender but still intact. Stir in spinach and cook until spinach is wilted, about 5 minutes. Adjust the taste with salt and pepper. Sprinkle with toasted garlic and serve warm.

Nutrition Info:

Per Serving: Calories: 189;Fat: 5.5g;Protein: 9g;Carbs: 27.1g.

Curry Apple Couscous With Leeks And Pecans

Servings:4

Cooking Time: 8 Minutes

Ingredients:

- 2 teaspoons extra-virgin olive oil
- 2 leeks, white parts only, sliced
- 1 apple, diced
- 2 cups cooked couscous
- 2 tablespoons curry powder
- ½ cup chopped pecans

Directions:

1. Heat the olive oil in a skillet over medium heat until shimmering.
2. Add the leeks and sauté for 5 minutes or until soft.
3. Add the diced apple and cook for 3 more minutes until tender.
4. Add the couscous and curry powder. Stir to combine.
5. Transfer them in a large serving bowl, then mix in the pecans and serve.

Nutrition Info:

Per Serving: Calories: 254;Fat: 11.9g;Protein: 5.4g;Carbs: 34.3g.

Basic Brown Rice Pilaf With Capers

Servings:4

Cooking Time:30 Minutes

Ingredients:

- 2 tbsp olive oil
- 1 cup brown rice
- 1 onion, chopped
- 1 celery stalk, chopped
- 2 garlic cloves, minced
- ½ cup capers, rinsed
- Salt and black pepper to taste
- 2 tbsp parsley, chopped

Directions:

1. Warm the olive oil in a skillet over medium heat. Sauté celery, garlic, and onion for 10 minutes. Stir in rice, capers, 2 cups of water, salt, and pepper and cook for 25 minutes. Serve topped with parsley.

Nutrition Info:

Per Serving: Calories: 230;Fat: 8.9g;Protein: 7g;Carbs: 16g.

Marrakech-style Couscous

Servings:4

Cooking Time:25 Minutes

Ingredients:

- 2 tbsp olive oil
- 1 cup instant couscous
- 2 tbsp dried apricots, chopped
- 2 tbsp dried sultanas
- ½ onion, minced
- 1 orange, juiced and zested
- ¼ tsp paprika
- ¼ tsp turmeric
- ½ tsp garlic powder
- ½ tsp ground cumin
- ¼ tsp ground cinnamon
- Salt and black pepper to taste

Directions:

1. Warm olive oil in a pot over medium heat and sauté onion for 3 minutes. Add in orange juice, orange zest, garlic powder, cumin, salt, paprika, turmeric, cinnamon, black pepper, and 2 cups of water and bring to a boil. Stir in apricots, couscous, and sultanas. Remove from the heat and let sit covered for 5 minutes. Fluff the couscous using a fork. Serve.

Nutrition Info:

Per Serving: Calories: 246;Fat: 7.4g;Protein: 5g;Carbs: 41.8g.

Kale Chicken With Pappardelle

Servings:4

Cooking Time:30 Min + Chilling Time

Ingredients:

- 1 cup grated Parmigiano-Reggiano cheese
- 4 chicken thighs, cut into 1-inch pieces
- 3 tbsp olive oil
- 16 oz pappardelle pasta
- Salt and black pepper to taste
- 1 yellow onion, chopped
- 4 garlic cloves, minced
- 12 cherry tomatoes, halved
- ½ cup chicken broth
- 2 cups baby kale, chopped
- 2 tbsp pine nuts for topping

Directions:

1. In a pot of boiling water, cook the pappardelle pasta for 8-10 minutes until al dente. Drain and set aside.
2. Heat the olive oil in a medium pot. Season the chicken with salt and pepper and sear in the oil until golden brown on the outside. Transfer to a plate and set aside. Add the onion and garlic to the oil and cook until softened and fragrant, 3 minutes. Mix in tomatoes and chicken broth and cook over low heat until the tomatoes soften and the liquid reduces by half. Season with salt and pepper. Return the chicken to the pot and stir in kale. Allow wilting for 2 minutes. Spoon

the pappardelle onto serving plates, top with kale sauce and
Parmigianino-Reggiano cheese. Garnish with pine nuts.

Nutrition Info:

Per Serving: Calories: 740;Fat: 53g;Protein: 50g;Carbs: 15g.

Mashed Beans With Cumin

Servings:4

Cooking Time: 10 To 12 Minutes

Ingredients:

- 1 tablespoon extra-virgin olive oil, plus extra for serving
- 4 garlic cloves, minced
- 1 teaspoon ground cumin
- 2 cans fava beans
- 3 tablespoons tahini
- 2 tablespoons lemon juice, plus lemon wedges for serving
- Salt and pepper, to taste
- 1 tomato, cored and cut into ½-inch pieces
- 1 small onion, chopped finely
- 2 hard-cooked large eggs, chopped
- 2 tablespoons minced fresh parsley

Directions:

1. Add the olive oil, garlic and cumin to a medium saucepan over medium heat. Cook for about 2 minutes, or until fragrant.
2. Stir in the beans with their liquid and tahini. Bring to a simmer and cook for 8 to 10 minutes, or until the liquid thickens slightly.
3. Turn off the heat, mash the beans to a coarse consistency with a potato masher. Stir in the lemon juice and 1 teaspoon pepper. Season with salt and pepper.

4. Transfer the mashed beans to a serving dish. Top with the tomato, onion, eggs and parsley. Drizzle with the extra olive oil.

5. Serve with the lemon wedges.

Nutrition Info:

Per Serving: Calories: 125;Fat: 8.6g;Protein: 4.9g;Carbs: 9.1g.

Mustard Vegetable Millet

Servings:6

Cooking Time:35 Minutes

Ingredients:

- 6 oz okra, cut into 1-inch lengths
- 3 tbsp olive oil
- 6 oz asparagus, chopped
- Salt and black pepper to taste
- 1 ½ cups whole millet
- 2 tbsp lemon juice
- 2 tbsp minced shallot
- 1 tsp Dijon mustard
- 6 oz cherry tomatoes, halved
- 3 tbsp chopped fresh dill
- 2 oz goat cheese, crumbled

Directions:

1. In a large pot, bring 4 quarts of water to a boil. Add asparagus, snap peas, and salt and cook until crisp-tender, about 3 minutes. Using a slotted spoon, transfer vegetables to a large plate and let cool completely, about 15 minutes. Add millet to water, return to a boil, and cook until grains are tender, 15-20 minutes.
2. Drain millet, spread in rimmed baking sheet, and let cool completely, 15 minutes. Whisk oil, lemon juice, shallot, mustard, salt, and pepper in a large bowl. Add vegetables, millet, tomatoes, dill, and half of the goat cheese and toss

gently to combine. Season with salt and pepper. Sprinkle with remaining goat cheese to serve.

Nutrition Info:

Per Serving: Calories: 315;Fat: 19g;Protein: 13g;Carbs: 35g.

Caprese Pasta With Roasted Asparagus

Servings:6

Cooking Time: 25 Minutes

Ingredients:

- 8 ounces uncooked small pasta, like orecchiette (little ears) or farfalle (bow ties)
- 1½ pounds fresh asparagus, ends trimmed and stalks chopped into 1-inch pieces
- 1½ cups grape tomatoes, halved
- 2 tablespoons extra-virgin olive oil
- ¼ teaspoon kosher salt
- ¼ teaspoon freshly ground black pepper
- 2 cups fresh Mozzarella, drained and cut into bite-size pieces
- $\frac{1}{3}$ cup torn fresh basil leaves
- 2 tablespoons balsamic vinegar

Directions:

1. Preheat the oven to 400ºF.
2. In a large stockpot of salted water, cook the pasta for about 8 to 10 minutes. Drain and reserve about ¼ cup of the cooking liquid.
3. Meanwhile, in a large bowl, toss together the asparagus, tomatoes, oil, salt and pepper. Spread the mixture onto a large, rimmed baking sheet and bake in the oven for 15 minutes, stirring twice during cooking.

4. Remove the vegetables from the oven and add the cooked pasta to the baking sheet. Mix with a few tablespoons of cooking liquid to help the sauce become smoother and the saucy vegetables stick to the pasta.
5. Gently mix in the Mozzarella and basil. Drizzle with the balsamic vinegar. Serve from the baking sheet or pour the pasta into a large bowl.

Nutrition Info:

Per Serving: Calories: 147;Fat: 3.0g;Protein: 16.0g;Carbs: 17.0g.

Rice And Blueberry Stuffed Sweet Potatoes

Servings:4

Cooking Time: 20 Minutes

Ingredients:

- 2 cups cooked wild rice
- ½ cup dried blueberries
- ½ cup chopped hazelnuts
- ½ cup shredded Swiss chard
- 1 teaspoon chopped fresh thyme
- 1 scallion, white and green parts, peeled and thinly sliced
- Sea salt and freshly ground black pepper, to taste
- 4 sweet potatoes, baked in the skin until tender

Directions:

1. Preheat the oven to 400ºF.
2. Combine all the ingredients, except for the sweet potatoes, in a large bowl. Stir to mix well.
3. Cut the top third of the sweet potato off length wire, then scoop most of the sweet potato flesh out.
4. Fill the potato with the wild rice mixture, then set the sweet potato on a greased baking sheet.
5. Bake in the preheated oven for 20 minutes or until the sweet potato skin is lightly charred.
6. Serve immediately.

Nutrition Info:

Per Serving: Calories: 393;Fat: 7.1g;Protein: 10.2g;Carbs: 76.9g.

Garlic And Parsley Chickpeas

Servings:4

Cooking Time: 18 To 20 Minutes

Ingredients:

- ¼ cup extra-virgin olive oil, divided
- 4 garlic cloves, sliced thinly
- ⅛ teaspoon red pepper flakes
- 1 onion, chopped finely
- ¼ teaspoon salt, plus more to taste
- Black pepper, to taste
- 2 cans chickpeas, rinsed
- 1 cup vegetable broth
- 2 tablespoons minced fresh parsley
- 2 teaspoons lemon juice

Directions:

1. Add 3 tablespoons of the olive oil, garlic, and pepper flakes to a skillet over medium heat. Cook for about 3 minutes, stirring constantly, or until the garlic turns golden but not brown.
2. Stir in the onion and ¼ teaspoon salt and cook for 5 to 7 minutes, or until softened and lightly browned.
3. Add the chickpeas and broth to the skillet and bring to a simmer. Reduce the heat to medium-low, cover, and cook for about 7 minutes, or until the chickpeas are cooked through and flavors meld.

4. Uncover, increase the heat to high and continue to cook for about 3 minutes more, or until nearly all liquid has evaporated.

5. Turn off the heat, stir in the parsley and lemon juice. Season to taste with salt and pepper and drizzle with remaining 1 tablespoon of the olive oil.

6. Serve warm.

Nutrition Info:

Per Serving: Calories: 220;Fat: 11.4g;Protein: 6.5g;Carbs: 24.6g.

Quinoa & Watercress Salad With Nuts

Servings:4

Cooking Time:5 Minutes

Ingredients:

- 2 boiled eggs, cut into wedges
- 2 cups watercress
- 2 cups cherry tomatoes, halved
- 1 cucumber, sliced
- 1 cup quinoa, cooked
- 1 cup almonds, chopped
- 2 tbsp olive oil
- 1 avocado, peeled and sliced
- 2 tbsp fresh cilantro, chopped
- Salt to taste
- 1 lemon, juiced

Directions:

1. Place watercress, cherry tomatoes, cucumber, quinoa, almonds, olive oil, cilantro, salt, and lemon juice in a bowl and toss to combine. Top with egg wedges and avocado slices and serve immediately.

Nutrition Info:

Per Serving: Calories: 530;Fat: 35g;Protein: 20g;Carbs: 45g.

Baked Rolled Oat With Pears And Pecans

Servings:6

Cooking Time: 30 Minutes

Ingredients:

- 2 tablespoons coconut oil, melted, plus more for greasing the pan
- 3 ripe pears, cored and diced
- 2 cups unsweetened almond milk
- 1 tablespoon pure vanilla extract
- ¼ cup pure maple syrup
- 2 cups gluten-free rolled oats
- ½ cup raisins
- ¾ cup chopped pecans
- ¼ teaspoon ground nutmeg
- teaspoon ground cinnamon
- ½ teaspoon ground ginger
- ¼ teaspoon sea salt

Directions:

1. Preheat the oven to 350ºF. Grease a baking dish with melted coconut oil, then spread the pears in a single layer on the baking dish evenly.
2. Combine the almond milk, vanilla extract, maple syrup, and coconut oil in a bowl. Stir to mix well.
3. Combine the remaining ingredients in a separate large bowl. Stir to mix well. Fold the almond milk mixture in the bowl, then pour the mixture over the pears.

4. Place the baking dish in the preheated oven and bake for 30 minutes or until lightly browned and set.
5. Serve immediately.

Nutrition Info:

Per Serving: Calories: 479;Fat: 34.9g;Protein: 8.8g;Carbs: 50.1g.

Autumn Vegetable & Rigatoni Bake

Servings:6

Cooking Time:45 Minutes

Ingredients:

- 2 tbsp grated Pecorino-Romano cheese
- 2 tbsp olive oil
- 1 lb pumpkin, chopped
- 1 zucchini, chopped
- 1 onion, chopped
- 1 lb rigatoni
- Salt and black pepper to taste
- ½ tsp garlic powder
- ½ cup dry white wine

Directions:

1. Preheat oven to 420 F. Combine zucchini, pumpkin, onion, and olive oil in a bowl. Arrange on a lined aluminum foil sheet and season with salt, pepper, and garlic powder. Bake for 30 minutes until tender. In a pot of boiling water, cook rigatoni for 8-10 minutes until al dente. Drain and set aside.
2. In a food processor, place ½ cup of the roasted veggies and wine and pulse until smooth.
3. Transfer to a skillet over medium heat. Stir in rigatoni and cook until heated through. Top with the remaining vegetables and Pecorino cheese to serve.

Nutrition Info:
Per Serving: Calories: 186;Fat: 11g;Protein: 10g;Carbs: 15g.

Simple Green Rice

Servings:4

Cooking Time:35 Minutes

Ingredients:

- 2 tbsp butter
- 4 spring onions, sliced
- 1 leek, sliced
- 1 medium zucchini, chopped
- 5 oz broccoli florets
- 2 oz curly kale
- ½ cup frozen green peas
- 2 cloves garlic, minced
- 1 thyme sprig, chopped
- 1 rosemary sprig, chopped
- 1 cup white rice
- 2 cups vegetable broth
- 1 large tomato, chopped
- 2 oz Kalamata olives, sliced

Directions:

1. Melt the butter in a saucepan over medium heat. Cook the spring onions, leek, and zucchini for about 4-5 minutes or until tender. Add in the garlic, thyme, and rosemary and continue to sauté for about 1 minute or until aromatic. Add in the rice, broth, and tomato. Bring to a boil, turn the heat to a gentle simmer, and cook for about 10-12 minutes. Stir in broccoli, kale, and green peas, and continue cooking for 5 minutes. Fluff the rice with a fork and garnish with olives.

Nutrition Info:

Per Serving: Calories: 403;Fat: 11g;Protein: 9g;Carbs: 64g.

Poultry And Meats

Sautéed Ground Turkey With Brown Rice

Servings:2

Cooking Time: 45 Minutes

Ingredients:

- 1 tablespoon olive oil
- ½ medium onion, minced
- 2 garlic cloves, minced
- 8 ounces ground turkey breast
- ½ cup chopped roasted red peppers,
- ¼ cup sun-dried tomatoes, minced
- 1¼ cups low-sodium chicken stock
- ½ cup brown rice
- 1 teaspoon dried oregano
- Salt, to taste
- 2 cups lightly packed baby spinach

Directions:

1. In a skillet, heat the olive oil over medium heat. Sauté the onion for 5 minutes, stirring occasionally.
2. Stir in the garlic and sauté for 30 seconds more until fragrant.
3. Add the turkey breast and cook for about 7 minutes, breaking apart with a wooden spoon, until the turkey is no longer pink.
4. Stir in the roasted red peppers, tomatoes, chicken stock, brown rice, and oregano and bring to a boil.

5. When the mixture starts to boil, cover, and reduce the heat to medium-low. Bring to a simmer until the rice is tender, stirring occasionally, about 30 minutes. Sprinkle with the salt.
6. Add the baby spinach and keep stirring until wilted.
7. Remove from the heat and serve warm.

Nutrition Info:

Per Serving: Calories: 445;Fat: 16.8g;Protein: 30.2g;Carbs: 48.9g.

Beef & Bell Pepper Bake

Servings:4

Cooking Time:1 Hour 40 Minutes

Ingredients:

- 2 tbsp olive oil
- 1 lb beef steaks
- 1 red bell pepper, sliced
- 1 green bell pepper, sliced
- 1 yellow bell pepper, sliced
- 2 tbsp oregano, chopped
- 4 garlic cloves, minced
- ½ cup chicken stock
- Salt and black pepper to taste

Directions:

1. Preheat oven to 360 F. Warm olive oil in a skillet over medium heat. Sear the beef steaks for 8 minutes on both sides. Stir in bell peppers, oregano, garlic, stock, salt, and pepper and bake for 80 minutes. Serve warm.

Nutrition Info:

Per Serving: Calories: 310;Fat: 15g;Protein: 25g;Carbs: 17g.

Pork & Vegetable Gratin

Servings:4

Cooking Time:40 Minutes

Ingredients:

- 3 tbsp olive oil
- 1 lb pork chops
- ½ cup basil leaves, chopped
- ½ cup mint leaves, chopped
- 1 tbsp rosemary, chopped
- 2 garlic cloves, minced
- 1 eggplant, cubed
- 2 zucchinis, cubed
- 1 bell pepper, chopped
- 2 oz mozzarella, crumbled
- 8 oz cherry tomatoes, halved

Directions:

1. Preheat the oven to 380 F. Place pork chops, basil, mint, rosemary, garlic, olive oil, eggplant, zucchinis, bell pepper, and tomatoes in a roasting pan and bake covered with foil for 27 minutes. Uncover, sprinkle with the mozzarella cheese, and bake for another 5-10 minutes until the cheese melts.

Nutrition Info:

Per Serving: Calories: 340;Fat: 18g;Protein: 25g;Carbs: 19g.

Dragon Pork Chops With Pickle Topping

Servings:4

Cooking Time:30 Minutes

Ingredients:

- ½ cup roasted bell peppers, chopped
- 6 dill pickles, sliced
- 1 cup dill pickle juice
- 6 pork chops, boneless
- Salt and black pepper to taste
- 1 tsp hot pepper sauce
- 1 ½ cups tomatoes, cubed
- 1 jalapeno pepper, chopped
- 10 black olives, sliced

Directions:

1. Place pork chops, hot sauce, and pickle juice in a bowl and marinate in the fridge for 15 minutes. Preheat your grill to High. Remove the chops from the fridge and grill them for 14 minutes on both sides. Combine dill pickles, tomatoes, jalapeño pepper, roasted peppers, and black olives in a bowl. Serve chops topped with the pickle mixture.

Nutrition Info:

Per Serving: Calories: 230;Fat: 7g;Protein: 36g;Carbs: 7g

Roasted Pork Tenderloin With Apple Sauce

Servings:4

Cooking Time:35 Minutes

Ingredients:

- 2 tbsp olive oil
- 1 lb pork tenderloin
- Salt and black pepper to taste
- ¼ cup apple jelly
- ¼ cup apple juice
- 2 tbsp wholegrain mustard
- 3 sprigs fresh thyme
- ½ tbsp cornstarch
- ½ tbsp heavy cream

Directions:

1. Preheat oven to 330 F. Warm the oil in a skillet over medium heat. Season the pork with salt and pepper. Sear it for 6-8 minutes on all sides. Transfer to a baking sheet. To the same skillet, add the apple jelly, juice, and mustard and stir for 5 minutes over low heat, stirring often. Top with the pork and thyme sprigs. Place the skillet in the oven and bake for 15-18 minutes, brushing the pork with the apple-mustard sauce every 5 minutes. Remove the pork and let it rest for 15 minutes. Place a small pot over low heat. Blend the cornstarch with heavy cream and cooking juices and pour the mixture into the pot. Stir for 2 minutes

until thickens. Drizzle the sauce over the pork. Serve sliced and enjoy!

Nutrition Info:

Per Serving: Calories: 146;Fat: 7g;Protein: 13g;Carbs: 8g.

Chicken Balls With Yogurt-cucumber Sauce

Servings:4

Cooking Time:40 Minutes

Ingredients:

- 3 tbsp olive oil
- 2 garlic cloves, minced
- 1 lb ground chicken
- 1 egg
- 1 red onion, chopped
- ¼ tsp red pepper flakes
- ½ tsp dried oregano
- 1 cup Greek yogurt
- 1 cucumber, shredded
- ¼ tsp garlic powder
- 2 tbsp lemon juice
- 2 tbsp dill, chopped

Directions:

1. In a bowl, combine ground chicken, egg, red onion, garlic, oregano, and red pepper flakes. Mix to combine well and shape the mixture into 1-inch balls.
2. Preheat the oven to 360 F. Warm 2 tbsp of olive oil in a skillet over medium heat and brown the meatballs for 10 minutes on all sides. Transfer the meatballs to a baking dish and bake for another 15 minutes. Combine Greek yogurt, cucumber, remaining olive oil, garlic powder, lemon juice, and dill in a bowl. Serve the meatballs with yogurt sauce.

Nutrition Info:

Per Serving: Calories: 380;Fat: 17g;Protein: 24g;Carbs: 27g.

Crispy Pesto Chicken

Servings:2

Cooking Time: 50 Minutes

Ingredients:

- 12 ounces small red potatoes, scrubbed and diced into 1-inch pieces
- 1 tablespoon olive oil
- ½ teaspoon garlic powder
- ¼ teaspoon salt
- 1 boneless, skinless chicken breast
- 3 tablespoons prepared pesto

Directions:

1. Preheat the oven to 425ºF. Line a baking sheet with parchment paper.
2. Combine the potatoes, olive oil, garlic powder, and salt in a medium bowl. Toss well to coat.
3. Arrange the potatoes on the parchment paper and roast for 10 minutes. Flip the potatoes and roast for an additional 10 minutes.
4. Meanwhile, put the chicken in the same bowl and toss with the pesto, coating the chicken evenly.
5. Check the potatoes to make sure they are golden brown on the top and bottom. Toss them again and add the chicken breast to the pan.
6. Turn the heat down to 350ºF and roast the chicken and potatoes for 30 minutes. Check to make sure the chicken reaches an internal temperature of 165ºF and the potatoes are fork-tender.

7.   Let cool for 5 minutes before serving.

Nutrition Info:

Per Serving: Calories: 378;Fat: 16.0g;Protein: 29.8g;Carbs: 30.1g.

Panko Grilled Chicken Patties

Servings:4

Cooking Time: 8 To 10 Minutes

Ingredients:

- 1 pound ground chicken
- 3 tablespoons crumbled feta cheese
- 3 tablespoons finely chopped red pepper
- ¼ cup finely chopped red onion
- 3 tablespoons panko bread crumbs
- 1 garlic clove, minced
- 1 teaspoon chopped fresh oregano
- ¼ teaspoon salt
- ⅛ teaspoon freshly ground black pepper
- Cooking spray

Directions:

1. Mix together the ground chicken, feta cheese, red pepper, red onion, bread crumbs, garlic, oregano, salt, and black pepper in a large bowl, and stir to incorporate.
2. Divide the chicken mixture into 8 equal portions and form each portion into a patty with your hands.
3. Preheat a grill to medium-high heat and oil the grill grates with cooking spray.
4. Arrange the patties on the grill grates and grill each side for 4 to 5 minutes, or until the patties are cooked through.
5. Rest for 5 minutes before serving.

Nutrition Info:

Per Serving: Calories: 241;Fat: 13.5g;Protein: 23.2g;Carbs: 6.7g.

Greek-style Chicken & Egg Bake

Servings:4

Cooking Time:45 Minutes

Ingredients:

- ½ lb Halloumi cheese, grated
- 1 tbsp olive oil
- 1 lb chicken breasts, cubed
- 4 eggs, beaten
- 1 tsp dry mustard
- 2 cloves garlic, crushed
- 2 red bell peppers, sliced
- 1 red onion, sliced
- 2 tomatoes, chopped
- 1 tsp sweet paprika
- ½ tsp dried basil
- Salt to taste

Directions:

1. Preheat oven to 360 F. Warm the olive oil in a skillet over medium heat. Add the bell peppers, garlic, onion, and salt and cook for 3 minutes. Stir in tomatoes for an additional 5 minutes. Put in chicken breasts, paprika, dry mustard, and basil. Cook for another 6-8 minutes. Transfer the mixture to a greased baking pan and pour over the beaten eggs; season with salt. Bake for 15-18 minutes. Remove and spread the cheese over the top. Let cool for a few minutes. Serve sliced.

Nutrition Info:

Per Serving: Calories: 480;Fat: 31g;Protein: 39g;Carbs: 12g.

Chicken Thighs With Roasted Artichokes

Servings:4

Cooking Time:25 Minutes

Ingredients:

- 2 artichoke hearts, halved lengthwise
- 2 tbsp butter, melted
- 3 tbsp olive oil
- 2 lemons, zested and juiced
- ½ tsp salt
- 4 chicken thighs

Directions:

1. Preheat oven to 450 F. Place a large, rimmed baking sheet in the oven. Whisk the olive oil, lemon zest, and lemon juice in a bowl. Add the artichoke hearts and turn them to coat on all sides. Lay the artichoke halves flat-side down in the center of 4 aluminum foil sheets and close up loosely to create packets. Put the chicken in the remaining lemon mixture and toss to coat. Carefully remove the hot baking sheet from the oven and pour on the butter; tilt the pan to coat.

2. Arrange the chicken thighs, skin-side down, on the sheet, add the artichoke packets. Roast for about 20 minutes or until the chicken is cooked through and the skin is slightly charred. Check the artichokes for doneness and bake for another 5 minutes if needed. Serve and enjoy!

Nutrition Info:

Per Serving: Calories: 832;Fat: 80g;Protein: 19g;Carbs: 11g.

Parsley-dijon Chicken And Potatoes

Servings:6

Cooking Time: 22 Minutes

Ingredients:

- 1 tablespoon extra-virgin olive oil
- 1½ pounds boneless, skinless chicken thighs, cut into 1-inch cubes, patted dry
- 1½ pounds Yukon Gold potatoes, unpeeled, cut into ½-inch cubes
- 2 garlic cloves, minced
- ¼ cup dry white wine
- 1 cup low-sodium or no-salt-added chicken broth
- 1 tablespoon Dijon mustard
- ¼ teaspoon freshly ground black pepper
- ¼ teaspoon kosher or sea salt
- 1 cup chopped fresh flat-leaf (Italian) parsley, including stems
- 1 tablespoon freshly squeezed lemon juice

Directions:

1. In a large skillet over medium-high heat, heat the oil. Add the chicken and cook for 5 minutes, stirring only after the chicken has browned on one side. Remove the chicken and reserve on a plate.

2. Add the potatoes to the skillet and cook for 5 minutes, stirring only after the potatoes have become golden and crispy on one side. Push the potatoes to the side of the skillet, add the garlic, and cook, stirring constantly, for 1

minute. Add the wine and cook for 1 minute, until nearly evaporated. Add the chicken broth, mustard, salt, pepper, and reserved chicken. Turn the heat to high and bring to a boil.

3. Once boiling, cover, reduce the heat to medium-low, and cook for 10 to 12 minutes, until the potatoes are tender and the internal temperature of the chicken measures 165ºF on a meat thermometer and any juices run clear.

4. During the last minute of cooking, stir in the parsley. Remove from the heat, stir in the lemon juice, and serve.

Nutrition Info:

Per Serving: Calories: 324;Fat: 9.0g;Protein: 16.0g;Carbs: 45.0g.

Rosemary Fennel In Cherry Tomato Sauce

Servings:4

Cooking Time:20 Minutes

Ingredients:

- 2 tbsp olive oil
- ½ tsp garlic, minced
- Salt and black pepper to taste
- ¼ cup vegetable broth
- 1 fennel, thinly sliced
- For the Sauce:
- 1 cup cherry tomatoes
- 2 tbsp fresh basil, chopped
- 1 tsp rosemary
- ½ cup red onion, chopped
- 1 tsp oregano
- 2 tbsp olive oil
- 1 cloves garlic, minced
- 1 cayenne pepper, minced
- Salt and black pepper to taste

Directions:

1. Warm the olive oil in a pan over medium heat. Sauté the

   garlic until aromatic. Add in the fennel, broth, salt, and pepper and cook until the fennel is just tender; remove to a plate. Puree the sauce ingredients in your food processor until smooth and creamy. Pour the sauce into a pan over medium heat and cook for 5-6 minutes. Pour the sauce over the fennel and serve.

Nutrition Info:

Per Serving: Calories: 138;Fat: 14g;Protein: 1g;Carbs: 3g.

Thyme Zucchini & Chicken Stir-fry

Servings:4

Cooking Time:40 Minutes

Ingredients:

- 2 tbsp olive oil
- 2 cups tomatoes, crushed
- 1 lb chicken breasts, cubed
- Salt and black pepper to taste
- 2 shallots, sliced
- 3 garlic cloves, minced
- 2 zucchinis, sliced
- 2 tbsp thyme, chopped
- 1 cup chicken stock

Directions:

1. Warm the olive oil in a skillet over medium heat. Sear chicken for 6 minutes, stirring occasionally. Add in shallots and garlic and cook for another 4 minutes. Stir in tomatoes, salt, pepper, zucchinis, and stock and bring to a boil; simmer for 20 minutes. Garnish with thyme and serve.

Nutrition Info:

Per Serving: Calories: 240;Fat: 10g;Protein: 19g;Carbs: 17g.

Easy Grilled Pork Chops

Servings:4

Cooking Time: 10 Minutes

Ingredients:

- ¼ cup extra-virgin olive oil
- 2 tablespoons fresh thyme leaves
- 1 teaspoon smoked paprika
- 1 teaspoon salt
- 4 pork loin chops, ½-inch-thick

Directions:

1. In a small bowl, mix together the olive oil, thyme, paprika, and salt.
2. Put the pork chops in a plastic zip-top bag or a bowl and coat them with the spice mix. Let them marinate for 15 minutes.
3. Preheat the grill to high heat. Cook the pork chops for 4 minutes on each side until cooked through.
4. Serve warm.

Nutrition Info:

Per Serving: Calories: 282;Fat: 23.0g;Protein: 21.0g;Carbs: 1.0g.

Ground Beef, Tomato, And Kidney Bean Chili

Servings:4

Cooking Time: 15 Minutes

Ingredients:

- 1 tablespoon extra-virgin olive oil
- 1 pound extra-lean ground beef
- 1 onion, chopped
- 2 cans kidney beans
- 2 cans chopped tomatoes, juice reserved
- Simple Chili Spice:
- 1 teaspoon garlic powder
- 1 tablespoon chili powder
- ½ teaspoon sea salt

Directions:

1. Heat the olive oil in a pot over medium-high heat until shimmering.
2. Add the beef and onion to the pot and sauté for 5 minutes or until the beef is lightly browned and the onion is translucent.
3. Add the remaining ingredients. Bring to a boil. Reduce the heat to medium and cook for 10 more minutes. Keep stirring during the cooking.
4. Pour them in a large serving bowl and serve immediately.

Nutrition Info:

Per Serving: Calories: 891;Fat: 20.1g;Protein: 116.3g;Carbs: 62.9g.

Lamb Tagine With Couscous And Almonds

Servings:6

Cooking Time: 7 Hours 7 Minutes

Ingredients:

- 2 tablespoons almond flour
- Juice and zest of 1 navel orange
- 2 tablespoons extra-virgin olive oil
- 2 pounds boneless lamb leg, fat trimmed and cut into 1½-inch cubes
- ½ cup low-sodium chicken stock
- 2 large white onions, chopped
- 1 teaspoon pumpkin pie spice
- ¼ teaspoon crushed saffron threads
- 1 teaspoon ground cumin
- ¼ teaspoon ground red pepper flakes
- ½ teaspoon sea salt
- 2 tablespoons raw honey
- 1 cup pitted dates
- 3 cups cooked couscous, for serving
- 2 tablespoons toasted slivered almonds, for serving

Directions:

1. Combine the almond flour with orange juice in a large bowl. Stir until smooth, then mix in the orange zest. Set aside.
2. Heat the olive oil in a nonstick skillet over medium-high heat until shimmering.

3. Add the lamb cubes and sauté for 7 minutes or until lightly browned.
4. Pour in the flour mixture and chicken stock, then add the onions, pumpkin pie spice, saffron, cumin, ground red pepper flakes, and salt. Stir to mix well.
5. Pour them in the slow cooker. Cover and cook on low for 6 hours or until the internal temperature of the lamb reaches at least 145ºF.
6. When the cooking is complete, mix in the honey and dates, then cook for another an hour.
7. Put the couscous in a tagine bowl or a simple large bowl, then top with lamb mixture. Scatter with slivered almonds and serve immediately.

Nutrition Info:

Per Serving: Calories: 447;Fat: 10.2g;Protein: 36.3g;Carbs: 53.5g.

Catalan Chicken In Romesco Sauce

Servings:6

Cooking Time:25 Minutes

Ingredients:

- 1 ½ lb chicken breasts, sliced
- 1 carrot, halved
- 1 celery stalk, halved
- 2 shallots, halved
- 2 garlic cloves, smashed
- 3 sprigs fresh thyme
- 1 cup romesco sauce
- 2 tbsp parsley, chopped
- ¼ tsp black pepper

Directions:

1. Place the chicken in a saucepan, cover well with water, and add the carrot, celery, onion, garlic, and thyme. Bring to the boil, then turn down to low and poach for 10-15 minutes until cooked through with no pink showing. Remove the chicken from the saucepan and leave to cool for 5 minutes. Spread some romesco sauce on the bottom of a serving plate. Arrange the chicken slices on top, and drizzle with the remaining romesco sauce. Sprinkle the tops with parsley and black pepper. Serve and enjoy!

Nutrition Info:

Per Serving: Calories: 270;Fat: 11g;Protein: 13g;Carbs: 31g.

Portuguese-style Chicken Breasts

Servings:4

Cooking Time:45 Minutes

Ingredients:

- 2 tbsp avocado oil
- 1 lb chicken breasts, cubed
- Salt and black pepper to taste
- 1 red onion, chopped
- 15 oz canned chickpeas
- 15 oz canned tomatoes, diced
- 1 cup Kalamata olives, pitted and halved
- 2 tbsp lime juice
- 1 tsp cilantro, chopped

Directions:

1. Warm the olive oil in a pot over medium heat and sauté chicken and onion for 5 minutes. Put in salt, pepper, chickpeas, tomatoes, olives, lime juice, cilantro, and 2 cups of water. Cover with lid and bring to a boil, then reduce the heat and simmer for 30 minutes. Serve warm.

Nutrition Info:

Per Serving: Calories: 360;Fat: 16g;Protein: 28g;Carbs: 26g.

Spicy Mustard Pork Tenderloin

Servings:4

Cooking Time:30 Minutes

Ingredients:

- 2 tbsp olive oil
- 1 pork tenderloin
- 2 garlic cloves, minced
- ½ cup fresh parsley, chopped
- 1 tbsp rosemary, chopped
- 1 tbsp tarragon, chopped
- 3 tbsp stone-ground mustard
- ½ tsp cumin powder
- ½ chili pepper, minced
- Salt and black pepper to taste

Directions:

1. Preheat oven to 400 F. In a food processor, blend parsley, tarragon, rosemary, mustard, olive oil, chili pepper, cumin, salt, garlic, and pepper until smooth. Rub the mixture all over the pork and transfer onto a lined baking sheet. Bake in the oven for 20-25 minutes. Slice and serve.

Nutrition Info:
Per Serving: Calories: 970;Fat: 29g;Protein: 16g;Carbs: 2.6g.

Picante Beef Stew

Servings:4

Cooking Time:35 Minutes

Ingredients:

- 2 tbsp olive oil
- 1 carrot, chopped
- 4 potatoes, diced
- 1 tsp ground nutmeg
- ½ tsp cinnamon
- 1 lb beef stew meat, cubed
- ½ cup sweet chili sauce
- ½ cup vegetable stock
- 1 tbsp cilantro, chopped
- Salt and black pepper to taste

Directions:

1. Warm the olive oil in a skillet over medium heat and sear beef for 5 minutes. Stir in chili sauce, carrot, potatoes, stock, nutmeg, cinnamon, cilantro, salt, and pepper and bring to a boil. Cook for another 20 minutes. Serve immediately.

Nutrition Info:

Per Serving: Calories: 300;Fat: 22g;Protein: 20g;Carbs: 26g.

Coriander Pork Roast

Servings:4

Cooking Time:2 Hours 10 Minutes

Ingredients:

- 2 tbsp olive oil
- 2 lb pork loin roast, boneless
- Salt and black pepper to taste
- 2 garlic cloves, minced
- 1 tsp ground coriander
- 1 tbsp coriander seeds
- 2 tsp red pepper, crushed

Directions:

1. Preheat the oven to 360 F. Toss pork, salt, pepper, garlic, ground coriander, coriander seeds, red pepper, and olive oil in a roasting pan and bake for 2 hours. Serve sliced.

Nutrition Info:

Per Serving: Calories: 310;Fat: 5g;Protein: 16g;Carbs: 7g.

Saucy Turkey With Ricotta Cheese

Servings:4

Cooking Time:60 Minutes

Ingredients:

- 2 tbsp olive oil
- 1 turkey breast, cubed
- 1 ½ cups salsa verde
- Salt and black pepper to taste
- 4 oz ricotta cheese, crumbled
- 2 tbsp cilantro, chopped

Directions:

1. Preheat the oven to 380 F. Grease a roasting pan with oil. In a bowl, place turkey, salsa verde, salt, and pepper and toss to coat. Transfer to the roasting pan and bake for 50 minutes. Top with ricotta cheese and cilantro and serve.

Nutrition Info:

Per Serving: Calories: 340;Fat: 16g;Protein: 35g;Carbs: 23g.

Peppery Chicken Bake

Servings:4

Cooking Time:70 Minutes

Ingredients:

- 3 tbsp olive oil
- 1 lb chicken breasts, sliced
- 2 lb cherry tomatoes, halved
- 1 onion, chopped
- 3 garlic cloves, minced
- 3 red chili peppers, chopped
- ½ lemon, zested
- Salt and black pepper to taste

Directions:

1. Warm the olive oil in a skillet over medium heat and brown chicken for 8 minutes on both sides. Remove to a roasting pan. In the same skillet, add onion, garlic, and chili peppers and cook for 2 minutes. Pour the mixture over the chicken and toss to coat. Add in tomatoes, lemon zest, 1 cup of water, salt, and pepper. Bake for 45 minutes. Serve and enjoy!

Nutrition Info:

Per Serving: Calories: 280;Fat: 14g;Protein: 34g;Carbs: 25g.

Fennel Beef Ribs

Servings:4

Cooking Time:2 Hours 10 Minutes

Ingredients:

- 2 tbsp olive oil
- 2 lb beef ribs
- 2 garlic cloves, minced
- 1 onion, chopped
- ½ cup chicken stock
- 1 tbsp ground fennel seeds

Directions:

1. Preheat oven to 360 F. Mix garlic, onion, stock, olive oil, fennel seeds, and beef ribs in a roasting pan and bake for 2 hours. Serve hot with salad.

Nutrition Info:

Per Serving: Calories: 300;Fat: 10g;Protein: 25g;Carbs: 18g.

Milky Pork Stew

Servings:4

Cooking Time:50 Minutes

Ingredients:

- 1 tbsp avocado oil
- 1 ½ cups buttermilk
- 1 ½ lb pork meat, cubed
- 1 red onion, chopped
- 1 garlic clove, minced
- ½ cup chicken stock
- 2 tbsp hot paprika
- Salt and black pepper to taste
- 1 tbsp cilantro, chopped

Directions:

1. Warm the avocado oil in a pot over medium heat and sear pork for 5 minutes. Put in onion and garlic and cook for 5 minutes. Stir in stock, paprika, salt, pepper, and buttermilk and bring to a boil; cook for 30 minutes. Top with cilantro.

Nutrition Info:
Per Serving: Calories: 310;Fat: 10g;Protein: 23g;Carbs: 16g.

Grilled Beef With Mint-jalapeño Vinaigrette

Servings:4

Cooking Time:25 Minutes

Ingredients:

- 2 tbsp olive oil
- 1 lb beef steaks
- 3 jalapeños, chopped
- 2 tbsp balsamic vinegar
- 1 cup mint leaves, chopped
- Salt and black pepper to taste
- 1 tbsp sweet paprika

Directions:

1. Warm half of oil in a skillet over medium heat and sauté jalapeños, balsamic vinegar, mint, salt, pepper, and paprika for 5 minutes. Preheat the grill to high. Rub beef steaks with the remaining oil, salt, and pepper and grill for 6 minutes on both sides. Top with mint vinaigrette and serve.

Nutrition Info:

Per Serving: Calories: 320;Fat: 13g;Protein: 18g;Carbs: 19g.

Beef & Vegetable Stew

Servings:6

Cooking Time:and Total Time: 35 Minutes

Ingredients:

- 2 sweet potatoes, cut into chunks
- 2 lb beef meat for stew
- ¾ cup red wine
- 1 tbsp butter
- 6 oz tomato paste
- 6 oz baby carrots, chopped
- 1 onion, finely chopped
- Salt to taste
- 4 cups beef broth
- ½ cup green peas
- 1 tsp dried thyme
- 3 garlic cloves, crushed

Directions:

1. Heat the butter on Sauté in your Instant pot. Add beef and brown for 5-6 minutes. Add onions and garlic, and keep stirring for 3 more minutes. Add the remaining ingredients and seal the lid. Cook on Meat/Stew for 20 minutes on High pressure. Do a quick release and serve immediately.

Nutrition Info:

Per Serving: Calories: 470;Fat: 15g;Protein: 51g;Carbs: 27g.

Almond-crusted Chicken Tenders With Honey

Servings:4

Cooking Time: 20 Minutes

Ingredients:

- 1 tablespoon honey
- 1 tablespoon whole-grain or Dijon mustard
- ¼ teaspoon freshly ground black pepper
- ¼ teaspoon kosher or sea salt
- 1 pound boneless, skinless chicken breast tenders or tenderloins
- 1 cup almonds, roughly chopped
- Nonstick cooking spray

Directions:

1. Preheat the oven to 425ºF. Line a large, rimmed baking sheet with parchment paper. Place a wire cooling rack on the parchment-lined baking sheet, and spray the rack well with nonstick cooking spray.
2. In a large bowl, combine the honey, mustard, pepper, and salt. Add the chicken and toss gently to coat. Set aside.
3. Dump the almonds onto a large sheet of parchment paper and spread them out. Press the coated chicken tenders into the nuts until evenly coated on all sides. Place the chicken on the prepared wire rack.
4. Bake in the preheated oven for 15 to 20 minutes, or until the internal temperature of the chicken measures 165ºF on a meat thermometer and any juices run clear.
5. Cool for 5 minutes before serving.

Nutrition Info:

Per Serving: Calories: 222;Fat: 7.0g;Protein: 11.0g;Carbs: 29.0g.

Pork Chops In Wine Sauce

Servings:4

Cooking Time:30 Minutes

Ingredients:

- 2 tbsp olive oil
- 4 pork chops
- 1 cup red onion, sliced
- 10 black peppercorns, crushed
- ¼ cup vegetable stock
- ¼ cup dry white wine
- 2 garlic cloves, minced
- Salt to taste

Directions:

1. Warm the olive oil in a skillet over medium heat and sear pork chops for 8 minutes on both sides. Put in onion and garlic and cook for another 2 minutes. Mix in stock, wine, salt, and peppercorns and cook for 10 minutes, stirring often.

Nutrition Info:

Per Serving: Calories: 240;Fat: 10g;Protein: 25g;Carbs: 14g.

Fruits, Desserts And Snacks

Avocado & Salmon Stuffed Cucumbers

Servings:4

Cooking Time:10 Minutes

Ingredients:

- 1 tbsp extra-virgin olive oil
- 2 large cucumbers, peeled
- 1 can red salmon
- 1 ripe avocado, mashed
- 2 tbsp chopped fresh dill
- Salt and black pepper to taste

Directions:

1. Cut the cucumber into 1-inch-thick segments, and using a spoon, scrape seeds out of the center of each piece and stand up on a plate. In a bowl, mix the salmon, avocado, olive oil, lime zest and juice, dill, salt, and pepper, and blend until creamy. Spoon the salmon mixture into the center of each cucumber segment and serve chilled.

Nutrition Info:

Per Serving: Calories: 159;Fat: 11g;Protein: 9g;Carbs: 8g.

Poached Pears In Red Wine

Servings:4

Cooking Time:1 Hour 35 Minutes

Ingredients:

- 4 pears, peeled with stalk intact
- 2 cups red wine
- 8 whole cloves
- 1 cinnamon stick
- ½ tsp vanilla extract
- 2 tsp sugar
- Creme fraiche for garnish

Directions:

1. In a pot over low heat, mix red wine, cinnamon stick, cloves, vanilla, and sugar and bring to a simmer, stirring often until the sugar is dissolved. Add in the pears, make sure that they are submerged and poach them for 15-20 minutes.
2. Remove the pears to a platter and allow the liquid simmering over medium heat for 15 minutes until reduced by half and syrupy. Remove from the heat and let cool for 10 minutes. Drain to discard the spices, let cool, and pour over the pears. Top with creme fraiche and serve.

Nutrition Info:

Per Serving: Calories: 158;Fat: 1g;Protein: 2g;Carbs: 33g.

The Best Trail Mix

Servings:4

Cooking Time:20 Minutes

Ingredients:

- 1 tbsp olive oil
- 1 tbsp maple syrup
- 1 tsp vanilla
- ½ tsp paprika
- ½ tsp cardamom
- ½ tsp allspice
- 2 cups mixed, unsalted nuts
- ¼ cup sunflower seeds
- ½ cup dried apricots, diced
- ½ cup dried figs, diced
- Salt to taste

Directions:

1. Mix the olive oil, maple syrup, vanilla, cardamom, paprika, and allspice in a pan over medium heat. Stir to combine. Add the nuts and seeds and stir well to coat. Let the nuts and seeds toast for about 10 minutes, stirring often. Remove from the heat, and add the dried apricots and figs. Stir everything well and season with salt. Store in an airtight container.

Nutrition Info:

Per Serving: Calories: 261;Fat: 18g;Protein: 6g;Carbs: 23g.

Strawberry Parfait

Servings:2

Cooking Time:10 Minutes

Ingredients:

- ¾ cup Greek yogurt
- 1 tbsp cocoa powder
- ¼ cup strawberries, chopped
- 5 drops vanilla stevia

Directions:

1. Combine cocoa powder, strawberries, yogurt, and stevia in a bowl. Serve immediately.

Nutrition Info:

Per Serving: Calories: 210;Fat: 9g;Protein: 5g;Carbs: 8g.

Greek Yogurt Affogato With Pistachios

Servings:4

Cooking Time: 0 Minutes

Ingredients:

- 24 ounces vanilla Greek yogurt
- 2 teaspoons sugar
- 4 shots hot espresso
- 4 tablespoons chopped unsalted pistachios
- 4 tablespoons dark chocolate chips

Directions:

1. Spoon the yogurt into four bowls or tall glasses.
2. Mix ½ teaspoon of sugar into each of the espresso shots.
3. Pour one shot of the hot espresso over each bowl of yogurt.
4. Top each bowl with 1 tablespoon of the pistachios and 1 tablespoon of the chocolate chips and serve.

Nutrition Info:

Per Serving: Calories: 190;Fat: 6.0g;Protein: 20.0g;Carbs: 14.0g.

Balsamic Squash Wedges With Walnuts

Servings:4

Cooking Time:50 Minutes

Ingredients:

- 3 tbsp olive oil
- 1 lb butternut squash, peeled and cut into wedges
- 1 cup walnuts, chopped
- 1 tbsp chili paste
- 1 tbsp balsamic vinegar
- 1 tbsp chives, chopped

Directions:

1. Preheat the oven to 380 F. Line a baking sheet with parchment paper. Combine squash wedges, chili paste, olive oil, vinegar, and chives in a bowl and arrange on the sheet. Bake for 40 minutes, turning often. Sprinkle with walnuts.

Nutrition Info:

Per Serving: Calories: 190;Fat: 5g;Protein: 2g;Carbs: 7g.

Turkish Baklava

Servings:6

Cooking Time:40 Min + Chilling Time

Ingredients:

- 20 sheets phyllo pastry dough, at room temperature
- 1 cup butter, melted
- 1 ½ cups chopped walnuts
- 1 tsp ground cinnamon
- ¼ tsp ground cardamom
- ½ cup sugar
- ½ cup honey
- 2 tbsp lemon juice
- 1 tbsp lemon zest

Directions:

1. In a small pot, bring 1 cup of water, sugar, honey, lemon zest, and lemon juice just to a boil. Remove and let cool.
2. Preheat oven to 350 F. In a small bowl, mix the walnuts, cinnamon, and cardamom and set aside. Put the butter in a small bowl. Put 1 layer of phyllo dough on a baking sheet and slowly brush with butter. Carefully layer 2 more phyllo sheets, brushing each with butter in the baking pan and then layer 1 tbsp of the nut mix; layer 2 sheets and add another 1 tbsp of the nut mix; repeat with 2 sheets and nuts until you run out of nuts and dough, topping with the remaining phyllo dough sheets. Slice 4 lines into the baklava lengthwise and make another 4 or 5 slices diagonally across the pan. Bake for 30-40 minutes or until golden brown.

Remove the baklava from the oven and immediately cover it with the syrup. Let cool and serve.

Nutrition Info:

Per Serving: Calories: 443;Fat: 27g;Protein: 6g;Carbs: 47g.

Simple Peanut Butter And Chocolate Balls

Servings:15

Cooking Time: 0 Minutes

Ingredients:

- ¾ cup creamy peanut butter
- ¼ cup unsweetened cocoa powder
- 2 tablespoons softened almond butter
- ½ teaspoon vanilla extract
- 1¾ cups maple sugar

Directions:

1. Line a baking sheet with parchment paper.
2. Combine all the ingredients in a bowl. Stir to mix well.
3. Divide the mixture into 15 parts and shape each part into a 1-inch ball.
4. Arrange the balls on the baking sheet and refrigerate for at least 30 minutes, then serve chilled.

Nutrition Info:

Per Serving: Calories: 146;Fat: 8.1g;Protein: 4.2g;Carbs: 16.9g.

Easy Blueberry And Oat Crisp

Servings:4

Cooking Time: 20 Minutes

Ingredients:

- 2 tablespoons coconut oil, melted, plus additional for greasing
- 4 cups fresh blueberries
- Juice of ½ lemon
- 2 teaspoons lemon zest
- ¼ cup maple syrup
- 1 cup gluten-free rolled oats
- ½ cup chopped pecans
- ½ teaspoon ground cinnamon
- Sea salt, to taste

Directions:

1. Preheat the oven to 350ºF. Grease a baking sheet with coconut oil.
2. Combine the blueberries, lemon juice and zest, and maple syrup in a bowl. Stir to mix well, then spread the mixture on the baking sheet.
3. Combine the remaining ingredients in a small bowl. Stir to mix well. Pour the mixture over the blueberries mixture.
4. Bake in the preheated oven for 20 minutes or until the oats are golden brown.
5. Serve immediately with spoons.

Nutrition Info:

Per Serving: Calories: 496;Fat: 32.9g;Protein: 5.1g;Carbs: 50.8g.

Roasted Eggplant Hummus

Servings:4

Cooking Time:25 Minutes

Ingredients:

- 1 lb eggplants, peeled and sliced
- 1 lemon, juiced
- 1 garlic clove, minced
- ¼ cup tahini
- ¼ tsp ground cumin
- Salt and black pepper to taste
- 2 tbsp fresh parsley, chopped
- ½ cup mayonnaise

Directions:

1. Preheat oven to 350 F. Arrange the eggplant slices on a baking sheet and bake for 15 minutes until tender. Let cool slightly before chopping. In a food processor, mix eggplants, salt, lemon juice, tahini, cumin, garlic, and pepper for 30 seconds. Remove to a bowl. Stir in mayonnaise. Serve topped with parsley.

Nutrition Info:

Per Serving: Calories: 235;Fat: 18g;Protein: 4.1g;Carbs: 17g.

Turkish Dolma (stuffed Grape Leaves)

Servings:4

Cooking Time:50 Minutes

Ingredients:

- 2 tbsp olive oil
- 1 onion, chopped
- 2 garlic cloves, minced
- 1 cup short-grain rice
- ¼ cup gold raisins
- ¼ cup pine nuts, toasted
- 1 lemon, juiced
- ¼ tsp ground cinnamon
- Salt and black pepper to taste
- 2 tbsp parsley, chopped
- 20 preserved grape leaves

Directions:

1. Warm the olive oil in a skillet over medium heat. Add the onion and garlic and sauté for 5 minutes. Add the rice, golden raisins, pine nuts, cinnamon, and lemon juice. Season with salt and pepper. Stuff each leaf with about 1 tablespoon of the filling. Roll tightly and place each in a pot, seam side down. Add 2 cups of water and simmer for about 1518 minutes. Serve warm.

Nutrition Info:

Per Serving: Calories: 237;Fat: 12g;Protein: 7g;Carbs: 26g.

Chili Grilled Eggplant Rounds

Servings:4

Cooking Time:25 Minutes

Ingredients:

- 1 cup roasted peppers, chopped
- 4 tbsp olive oil
- 2 eggplants, cut into rounds
- 12 Kalamata olives, chopped
- 1 tsp red chili flakes, crushed
- Salt and black pepper to taste
- 2 tbsp basil, chopped
- 2 tbsp Parmesan cheese, grated

Directions:

1. Combine roasted peppers, half of the olive oil, olives, red chili flakes, salt, and pepper in a bowl. Rub each eggplant slice with remaining olive oil and salt grill them on the preheated grill for 14 minutes on both sides. Remove to a platter. Distribute the pepper mixture across the eggplant rounds and top with basil and Parmesan cheese to serve.

Nutrition Info:

Per Serving: Calories: 220;Fat: 11g;Protein: 6g;Carbs: 16g.

Vegetarian Spinach-olive Pizza

Servings:4

Cooking Time:40 Minutes

Ingredients:

- For the crust
- 1 tbsp olive oil
- ½ cup almond flour
- ¼ tsp salt
- 2 tbsp ground psyllium husk
- 1 cup lukewarm water
- For the topping
- ½ cup tomato sauce
- ½ cup baby spinach
- 1 cup grated mozzarella
- 1 tsp dried oregano
- 3 tbsp sliced black olives

Directions:

1. Preheat the oven to 400 F. Line a baking sheet with parchment paper. In a medium bowl, mix the almond flour, salt, psyllium powder, olive oil, and water until dough forms.

2. Spread the mixture on the pizza pan and bake in the oven until crusty, 10 minutes. When ready, remove the crust and spread the tomato sauce on top. Add the spinach, mozzarella cheese, oregano, and olives. Bake until the cheese melts, 15 minutes. Take out of the oven, slice and serve warm.

Nutrition Info:

Per Serving: Calories: 167;Fat: 13g;Protein: 4g;Carbs: 6.7g.

Spicy Roasted Chickpeas

Servings:2

Cooking Time:40 Minutes

Ingredients:

- Chickpeas
- 1 tbsp olive oil
- 1 can chickpeas
- Salt to taste
- Seasoning Mix
- ¾ tsp cumin
- ½ tsp ground coriander
- Salt and black pepper to taste
- ¼ tsp chili powder
- ½ tsp cayenne pepper
- ¼ tsp cardamom
- ¼ tsp cinnamon
- ¼ tsp allspice

Directions:

1. Preheat oven to 400 F. In a small bowl, place all the seasoning mix ingredients and stir well to combine.
2. Place the chickpeas in a bowl and season them with olive oil and salt. Add the chickpeas to a lined baking sheet and roast them for about 25-35 minutes, turning them over once or twice while cooking until they are slightly crisp. Remove to a bowl and sprinkle them with the seasoning mix. Toss lightly to combine. Serve and enjoy!

Nutrition Info:

Per Serving: Calories: 268;Fat: 11g;Protein: 11g;Carbs: 35g.

Speedy Granita

Servings:4

Cooking Time:10 Min + Freezing Time

Ingredients:

- ¼ cup sugar
- 1 cup fresh strawberries
- 1 cup fresh raspberries
- 1 cup chopped fresh kiwi
- 1 tsp lemon juice

Directions:

1. Bring 1 cup water to a boil in a small saucepan over high heat. Add the sugar and stir well until dissolved. Remove the pan from the heat, add the fruit and lemon juice, and cool to room temperature. Once cooled, puree the fruit in a blender until smooth. Pour the puree into a shallow glass baking dish and place in the freezer for 1 hour. Stir with a fork and freeze for 30 minutes, then repeat. Serve and enjoy!

Nutrition Info:

Per Serving: Calories: 153;Fat: 0.2g;Protein: 1.6g;Carbs: 39g.

Cantaloupe & Watermelon Balls

Servings:4

Cooking Time:5 Min + Chilling Time

Ingredients:

- 2 cups watermelon balls
- 2 cups cantaloupe balls
- ½ cup orange juice
- ¼ cup lemon juice
- 1 tbsp orange zest

Directions:

1. Place the watermelon and cantaloupe in a bowl. In another bowl, mix the lemon juice, orange juice and zest. Pour over the fruit. Transfer to the fridge covered for 5 hours. Serve.

Nutrition Info:

Per Serving: Calories: 71;Fat: 0g;Protein: 1.5g;Carbs: 18g.

Charred Asparagus

Servings:4

Cooking Time:25 Minutes

Ingredients:

- 2 tbsp olive oil
- 1 lb asparagus, trimmed
- 4 tbsp Grana Padano, grated
- ½ tsp garlic powder
- Salt to taste
- 2 tbsp parsley, chopped

Directions:

1. Preheat the grill to high. Season the asparagus with salt and garlic powder and coat with olive oil. Grill the asparagus for 10 minutes, turning often until lightly charred and tender. Sprinkle with cheese and parsley and serve.

Nutrition Info:

Per Serving: Calories: 105;Fat: 8g;Protein: 4.3g;Carbs: 4.7g.